PRACTICAL
TIDINESS

PRACTICAL
TIDINESS

———

How to clear your clutter
and make space for the
important things in life:
a room by room guide

MARTHA ROBERTS

LORENZ BOOKS

contents

Introduction

Tidiness is both a physical entity and a frame of mind. It's a global craze tapping into the human need for order, calm and sanctuary in a busy world. It takes time and effort to get organised but the results can be lifechanging.

Do you yearn to be surrounded by tidiness? Do you wish you could spend your days enjoying your home rather than endlessly searching through boxes, drawers and cupboards for something you'd hope to find in an instant? If so, you're not alone. Being tidier and more organised is something we all aspire to in some way – almost half of us say we even enjoy the process, and research shows that we spend an average of 7.5 hours per week tidying.

However, there appears to be gap between the desire for order and actually achieving it. A 2017 UK survey found that when asked to score whether they were 'seriously untidy', most people rated themselves between a 5 and an 8 out of 10: when it comes to being tidy, we don't rate ourselves very highly.

Research suggests that living amongst clutter and chaos can spill out into the rest of our lives, making us feel uneasy and even unwell. Around two-thirds of us feel that clutter is causing us stress and one-third of households argue about clutter at least once a week. That's a whole lot of angst for something we could actually do something about. And yet, experts also tell us that rigid order may get in the way of creativity. When we start looking more into the subject of tidiness, we begin to see that it's quite subjective.

In 1861, Isabella Beeton published *Mrs Beeton's Book of Household Management* and famously pronounced, 'A place for everything and everything in its place'. More than 150 years on, this philosophy is still something we aspire to as we try to organise our busy, space-limited, time-stretched lives. Knowing what we want to keep and where we want to keep it, as well as being aware of what we no longer need and how to separate out from it, both physically and psychologically – that's quite a challenge. Learning about tidiness, what it really means to us as individuals and how we can overcome obstacles to it, can also help us to adapt the principles as a code for living. Tidiness isn't just about the physical act of putting things where we feel they ought to be: it's also about how we view the spaces we live in, how we function within each and every room, and how it can enhance our lives to improve our usage of these spaces.

In other words, tidiness is about how improved order can help us to be the very best version of ourselves. But first, let us address what exactly tidiness is.

WHAT IS

Tidiness?

Tidying up

At some point in our lives, someone has almost certainly said to us, 'Right – it's time we tidied up round here.' Whether as a child, a teenager ('Your room is a tip!') or an adult, the pursuit of tidiness is, it seems, an inevitable part of life.

Definitions of tidiness largely focus on neatness, organisation and systems. The Oxford English Dictionary goes further, describing it as 'The condition or quality of having everything ordered and arranged in the right place.'

Many of us will have industriously cracked on with the job of tidying, only to have someone else say, 'Well, that isn't what *I'd* call tidy!' or 'I wouldn't have put that there…' Maybe we've even expressed these thoughts to someone ourselves.

Whether you're considering what is the right place and what constitutes having everything ordered, tidiness is quite personal. We often make assumptions about what 'the

'Organising is what you do before you do something, so that when you do it, it is not all mixed up.'
WINNIE THE POOH (A. A. MILNE)

right place is', based on logic or even convention about where things are 'supposed' to live in a home. However, even this is open to interpretation (you might keep tea towels in your kitchen but a friend keeps theirs in an upstairs linen cupboard: both are arguably 'right'). Why? You only have to court opinion, search online or browse a bookstore to realise there is going to be more than one method of introducing tidiness into your life.

Some systems urge you to purge while others suggest it's more self-nurturing to do it in small steps ('A little better is a little better', says Fay Wolf, founder of the decluttering business New Order). Then there are those that tell you to stop accumulating, start shedding and be a minimalist and, conversely, those that tell you if your maximalist possessions – what they might term 'clutter' – are part of your

creativity and a fundamental aspect of your personality, they ought to be accommodated into your tidiness regime. You'll find there are a number of different philosophies of tidiness on offer.

With so much wide-ranging opinion on tidiness, how exactly should you set about achieving it? For a system to work in practice it's about finding an approach that works for you. If you discover one that's intuitive and respects your personal needs, whether that means embracing your creativity or maxing out on minimalism, then you're more likely to stick to it.

In this book, when we talk about 'tidiness' or 'tidying' what we mean is 'organisation'

and 'order' as it means to you. We're giving you guidance but we're also aware that one size doesn't always fit all. In other words, one person's tidiness heaven is another person's tidiness hell! We're not here to tell you to throw everything out and to stop being attached to things that matter to you. Instead, we give you practical pointers on how to start, working through your home room by room to create order in your life in a humane and compassionate way. A balanced approach is important; there is a Finnish proverb that says, 'Happiness is a place between too little and too much', which could be a guideline to our tidying-up as well as for life.

Different philosophies of tidiness

There isn't one way to tidy your home, or to organise your life, and it can be enlightening to consider other approaches to see what strikes a particular chord for you. There are of course insights to be found in all of them.

The world is full of many different kinds of people, each of whom may be striving for order in a multitude of ways. Not all tidiness methods are the same: the aim may be a tidy space but the philosophy leading to it can be fundamentally different.

'Ancient principle' philosophies
These suggest a link between minimalising physical objects and achieving inner psychological calm. They incorporate principles of feng shui, Buddhism and mindfulness to achieve 'conscious' tidying. Examples include *A Monk's Guide to A*

Clean House and Mind by Shoukei Matsumoto, who says, 'Once you learn how to see how your inner turmoil manifests itself through your surroundings, you can reverse engineer this, mastering yourself by mastering the space in which you live.'

'You can't take it with you' philosophies
These look at tidying in readiness for getting older and not being encumbered by an excess of 'things'. Exponents say you don't have to wait until you are knocking on 50 to start. Examples include *The Gentle Art of Swedish Death Cleaning* by Margareta

Magnusson. 'You can always hope and wait for someone to want something in your home, but you cannot wait forever, and sometimes you must just give cherished things away with the wish that they end up with someone who will create new memories of their own.'

'Minimalist v maximalist' philosophies

Some see the embracing of clutter or even creative messiness as a tidiness principle in itself. Examples of this approach include *Messy: How to Be Creative and Resilient in a Tidy-Minded World* by Tim Harford. He says we are 'so seduced by the blandishments of tidiness that we fail to appreciate the virtues of the messy'.

'Mass purge' or 'bit-by-bit' philosophies

Will you tidy in one fell swoop or are you more likely to do it if it's in little bite-sized chunks? Some philosophies focus on purging all at once to get things straight while others say starting small is the way to tidy without feeling defeated. Examples include *The Life-Changing Magic of Tidying* by Marie Kondo and *Start With Your Sock Drawer and the Rest Will Follow* by Vicky Silverthorn. Marie Kondo says, 'Small changes transform our lives.'

'Stop caring quite so much' philosophies

We can't talk about different ways of tidying without including a mention of the option of simply not tidying up at all. Some people believe that happiness lies in cluttering more mindfully and not being so hung up on trying to buy or own less. Examples of this rather more laid-back tidying philosophy include *The Joy of Leaving Your Sh*t All Over The Place: The Art of Being Messy* by Jennifer McCartney.

The science of tidiness

How about if you were to discover that when it comes to keeping tidy, science isn't necessarily helping? There are at least three ways in which scientific principles may stand in the way of order and organisation.

How many times have you tidied up and got things in order, only to discover that within a matter of days – if not hours – things start to look messed up again? As chaos stealthily creeps in it's all too easy to give yourself a hard time about it. But there is science behind it.

'Entropy is just a fancy way of saying: things fall apart.'

DAN BROWN, *ORIGIN*

Entropy

The second law of thermodynamics talks about entropy, which is a measure of the possible arrangements that atoms in a system can have, and how, on every level in our world, whether you're talking atoms or paperwork, all things naturally tend towards a state of disorder and that reversing this tendency requires the input of energy. Molecular changes tend to push things towards disorder rather than order. That's why you need to put effort in to tidy, for it to stay that way!

The messy desk of genius?

Several brilliant minds worked on constantly messy desks. Einstein famously said, 'If a cluttered desk is a sign of a cluttered mind, then what are we to think of an empty desk?'

Newton's Law of Motion

However... hand in hand with this we have Newton's first law of motion, which states that still objects won't move unless you shift them and this requires energy. On an atomic level, an object is inevitably undergoing changes that will, over time, move it towards a state of disrepair and degradation that's eventually visible to the naked eye. But while this is happening these items are staying put – including ones you put down and mean to go back to when you next tidy up.

'Parkinson's Law'

Okay, this isn't real science, but according to Parkinson's Law (a humorous adage by political analyst C. Northcote Parkinson, based on the general gas law that molecules fill the volume they occupy), work expands to the time available. We might similarly observe that mess typically expands to fill the space. The more we have, the more we fill.

What does this 'science' mean for you as someone trying to keep things tidy in your home? In a nutshell, it shows that things are inclined to get messy, even when we have the best intentions of keeping them tidy, and that no matter how much space you have, you'll always fill it with extra things – and to keep them in some kind of order you have to put some effort in. Why? Quite simply, objects won't move to the right place by themselves. In fact, they rather like moving to the wrong place (as those trainers piled up by the front door or Lego under the coffee table show…). Social scientist Jon Crowe says, 'A living room doesn't spontaneously tidy itself... We need to invest effort to reverse the spread of disorder, and bring order to whatever degree of chaos has befallen our living space since we last made the effort to tidy up. We are essentially swimming against the natural tide of entropy.'

Add to this the fact that our homes are generally getting smaller and you can see how keeping ordered can feel like an uphill struggle.

So next time you criticise yourself (or, indeed, your loved ones) about being messy or disorganised, remember that things scientifically tend that way – and only making a concerted effort to move them will get them back to a state of order again. Do put work into tidying up but accept that tidying is all part of the natural way of things.

The psychology of tidiness

Tidiness isn't just about the action of clearing things up and putting things away. There's so much more to it than that, from our perceptions of 'What is tidy?' through to our attitude towards the process.

We know that tidiness does many things, from boosting optimism levels and self-esteem and fostering calmer relationships. What tidiness means to us as individuals speaks volumes about how we view the world and our place in it, as well as our relationship with objects, people and places. Like many things in life, our approach towards tidiness springs from a range of places, especially early experiences of order and organisation. Does the thought of tidying make your heart sink or leap? There's a great deal of psychology involved in it.

Tidiness and childhood

If we look back on our own childhood, we'll no doubt have memories of how the household was run. Maybe it was excessively tidy, with someone constantly telling you to clear up after yourself, or maybe it was chaotic with very few rules and structure. In all likelihood it was somewhere in the middle. You may have grumbled about having to put your dirty clothes in the washing basket but research shows that children actually crave this kind of structure, despite their protestations. It also shows that chaos impacts their ability to focus. A 2011 study found that if there were too many objects in a child's field of view it affected their ability to focus (poor focus can slow down learning in toddlers). Other research found that a messy environment can have an 'additive' effect on a child's poor behaviour – if there are already shortcomings in parenting, the mess and disorder only makes things worse. Whatever our childhood experiences, psychology has shown time and again that lack of order and tidiness in childhood can impact our early years and beyond.

Tidiness and trauma

We all have possessions we prize over others and wouldn't want to part with. It's when this turns into a compulsion and an inability to part with anything, that it can become problematic – and achieving tidiness a seeming impossibility. At the extreme end of this, there could be a cause: there are studies that show a link between hoarding behaviour and traumatic events, and Australian researchers found a link between hoarding and trauma in older people, after such events as losing a spouse or a child. Keeping hold of 'stuff' can act as a way of filling an emotional gap left by the trauma and so, conversely, getting rid of the items can trigger high anxiety levels. Some help is at hand for hoarders or those with extreme untidiness behaviours (look in the Resources section at the back of the book for further information).

Tidiness and health

You may well have heard the phrase, 'Tidy house, tidy mind'. Research certainly shows a link between tidiness and mental health. A 2010 study found that women who described their living spaces as 'cluttered' or full of 'unfinished projects' were more likely to be worn out and depressed than those with 'restful' or 'restorative' homes. Other research found that a messy bedroom can lead to a poor night's sleep and increased anxiety, and that those with more cluttered rooms took longer to fall asleep than those with tidy bedrooms (think how soundly you sleep in a hotel room!).

Conversely, people with clean homes and who engaged in regular dusting, cleaning and doing the laundry were found to be healthier than those with messy homes. The study's authors suggested that it could be that the physical effort of housework was keeping them healthy, but that good habits – such as being more active beyond the home – flowed from this sense of order and cleanliness. Research also shows that having a clean, organised and tidy environment decreases the levels of mistakes and accidents both at home and in the workplace.

It's clear how the concept of tidiness can be much more than it appears in terms of psychology. But how does order and organisation have a practical place in your own life; in other words, do you really need to tidy, and how?

Do you need to tidy?

Maybe it was this morning, maybe last week – or maybe your last tidy-up was so long ago you can't even put a time to it. Chances are your home is probably due a little tidy… or maybe even a big one. Is now, finally, the time to start?

You're ready to start tidying – right? Perhaps the current tidiness craze that's sweeping the globe has made you start to wonder what it's all about and whether your own space is working for you in its current state. Maybe a well-meaning friend gave this book to you as a gentle way of suggesting that now is the time for you to (literally) start getting your house in order…

We're not here to judge, whatever state of organisation or otherwise your space is in. We know how hard it can be. Whatever has brought you to this book or this book to you, you're here. Congratulations! See this as a nudge in the right direction towards becoming more organised, and learning a set of useful skills to make that happen – and then making it a habit.

Chaos and cortisol

A US study found that levels of the stress hormone cortisol were higher in women who described their home environment as chaotic or messy. Interestingly, men in the study seemed to be less chemically affected by mess and clutter.

Or, you might not be sure you're feeling ready to tidy, but that doesn't mean that you don't need to. You may look around and the answer is staring you in the face – there are kids' toys lying around like primary-coloured booby traps, towels languishing on the bathroom floor and bags of off-season clothes on the landing waiting to be put in the loft for storage. You might feel frustrated every time you open a kitchen drawer and hunt for the three items you use regularly that are buried amongst the other two dozen unused items. These very visible manifestations of the need for more order can be hard to ignore, screaming out 'Tidy me!' in no uncertain terms. However, it may also be that you simply can't even see that the time has come for more order and organisation. Life can get so frenetic that sorting things out might not even be on your agenda.

So, what do you think: do you need to tidy? Answering 'yes' to even one of these following questions is an indicator that you could benefit from a bit more tidiness and order. Any more than one suggests that instigating a system of tidying could improve not just your physical space but your headspace, too.

Does your environment make you happy?

When you look around your home, do you feel joy and lightness? Is it a case of 'heart leap' or is it more like 'heart sink'? Do you go from room to room thinking, 'I love how this looks and how it makes me feel'? Or does that process make you unhappy, ground down or even depressed?

Why you should tidy Your home should be your sanctuary and a space that supports you rather than one that presents you with extra hurdles. Other parts of your life may be challenging but at least if your home is ordered how you like it, you'll have somewhere that brings you serenity. It is not selfish to direct attention to your daily space; it will impact on how you deal with life.

Do you make excuses or feel embarrassed when people come round?

Have you ever heard yourself greeting a visitor to your home with the words, 'I'm so sorry it's such a mess – I've just got back from holiday', even though the holiday was actually three weeks before? Or maybe you refuse to let people go beyond the boundaries of one room because you know the others are a tip?

Why you should tidy Research in 2017 found that nearly half of people surveyed feel embarrassed by clutter in their home. Feeling ashamed about your space could be a sign that you know it's not truly representative of who you are and how you'd like people to see you. Tidying will enable you to have

Do you keep losing things?

Lost your phone again? You're not the only one. It is estimated that the average person loses at least 3,000 possessions in their lifetime, including 384 pens and 192 items of clothing. These are the most commonly misplaced items:

1. Keys
2. Phone
3. Pens (or other items of stationery)
4. Glasses or sunglasses
5. Remote controls
6. Money
7. Socks
8. Phone charger
9. Bank cards
10. Gloves
11. Umbrella
12. Headphones
13. Wallet
14. Lipstick or make-up
15. Memory sticks
16. Jewellery
17. Diary
18. Shoes or trainers
19. Watch
20. Hat

people round without it making you feel awkward and having to tell unsettling untruths. It will also make you feel happier (81 per cent of people say that tidying improves their mood).

Are you forever losing things or buying duplicates?

Have you ever packed to go on holiday and found yourself needing to buy yet another adaptor plug, even though you know you have at least four already? Do you have a chest of drawers that's so crammed full of clothes that you've forgotten what's lurking at the back of them? Do you find yourself saying 'Oh, I haven't seen that for years!' when you clear through cupboards?

Why you should tidy Research shows that we spend ten minutes each day searching for our lost items and most of us know that untidiness is to blame, with more than half of us wishing we were more organised. Losing things and needing to buy replacements is not only profligate but it's a clear indication that you don't have a sufficient organisational system in place. Tidying will mean you can find what you're after – and save money by not having to replace things.

Does your home make you feel calm?

When you visualise your home, does it fill you with a sense of tranquillity and peace? Is it a serene space that feels like a haven from the frenetic buzz of the outside world? Or is it somewhere that raises your blood pressure and makes you feel agitated?

Why you should tidy If your home makes you feel frazzled, chances are it's because there's too much visual 'noise'. Research in 2010 used linguistic analysis software to measure how 60 people discussed their homes. Those who described their spaces as 'cluttered' or full of 'unfinished projects' were more likely to be depressed and fatigued than those whose homes were 'restful' and 'restorative'.

Do you prefer to be in other people's places than your own?

If a friend says, 'Shall we meet for a coffee?', do you tend to suggest going to their place or even going out? Is it a case of 'Anywhere but mine!'? It may be that no sooner have you entered the front door you are filled with the desire to leave again.

Why you should tidy A study showed that nearly half of us (47 per cent) hide clutter from communal areas in bedrooms when expecting guests, knowing 'no-one will go in there'. Sometimes going to other people's homes seems preferable.

A constant need to spend time in other people's places rather than your own is an indicator that your own home is leaving you uninspired and could even be causing you irritation or distress. Getting tidy and organised could help you to fall in love with your space again.

Thinking CHAOS

Professional organisers often refer to this. CHAOS stands for 'Can't Have Anyone Over Syndrome'. If you find yourself not inviting guests over because you can't stand the mess, it could be time to act.

Do you find yourself wearing the same set of clothes?

Are there drawers you haven't seen the back of for months – or even years? When you choose your outfit, do you tend to reach for something that's in the front half of the drawer while the rest of its contents lie behind and undisturbed, hiding many clothes you probably don't remember even buying? Some of them won't fit or will be out of date, but some are sure to be wearable.

Why you should tidy You're wearing and cleaning the same items, over and over again, because you aren't given the visual prompt to wear anything else when you open your drawers. Knowing what's already in your chest of drawers and wardrobe will be good for your wallet (you won't be tempted to buy 'a useful white t-shirt' if you can see all the other ones you already have) and good for the environment, too.

Are you a maximalist or minimalist?

The concepts of maximalism and minimalism – a love of excess versus a love of less – were first talked about decades ago. However, it's only in recent years that they've been applied to interiors and how we live our life with 'things'.

Imagine this: you enter a home and the first thing you see is clean lines and empty spaces. There's nothing on the floor that shouldn't be there and as you move from room to room, everything is in cupboards or drawers and 'in its place'. If you had to describe it you might say it is 'calming'.

Now imagine this: you enter the same home, only this time it is filled with colours, shapes and 'stuff'. There are lots of objects on display, including ephemera and loved objects that are bursting with stories. There may be a system but to the naked eye it looks pretty random. If you had to describe it, the word 'disorganised' comes to mind.

This isn't an exercise in deciding which is best. When it comes to tidiness it's highly subjective. One person's minimalist perfection is another person's stark nightmare. On the other hand, one person's maximalist heaven is another person's cluttered hell. There is no right or wrong – just 'different'. It's about how you decide you like to live.

What are the differences between maximalists and minimalists when it comes to how they like to tidy, and can they live together? Are you and those you live with like peas in a pod, or chalk and cheese?

Minimalists love:
- Living with less ('I have what I need')
- Minimal visual clutter
- Empty spaces
- Clean lines
- Calming colours and patterns
- Minimal soft furnishings
- Fixed decor

Minimalist tidying:
- Purposeful
- Everything has a place
- Things are put away so they aren't constantly seen
- Surfaces are clear
- Embraces storage

Maximalists love:
- Living with more ('I don't really need it but I love it!')
- The joy of 'things', many brimming with life and history
- Spatial 'busyness'
- Being creative
- Bold colours and patterns
- Soft furnishings for comfort
- Seeing spaces as dynamic and evolving

Maximalist tidying:
- Accidental or incidental
- Surfaces may be busy – but styled

- Finding order within chaos (may be creative, perhaps colour-themed)
- Objects are easily accessible and ever-present, even if stowed away
- Storage is crucial, but likely to be quirky and with the purpose of displaying things

The art of compromise

Although you may live with someone or share a space because of your similarities, it may be you're very different when it comes to the way you organise that space. A maximalist and a minimalist living together doesn't have to be a recipe for disaster.

Discuss what 'tidy' means to you Make a list of general principles but also go through, room by room, saying how you'd like it to be. This way you can discover if you're on a similar page even if you have different styles.

Focus on your 'sameness' Harmonious living requires us to focus on what we have in common rather than our differences. What do you both like? This could include your joint love of plants, books or the desire to have your cocktail spirits on display.

Be compassionate It's easy to be self-righteous when it comes to tidying styles but we are the way we are for a reason. Perhaps you're a maximalist because you're visual, and not being able to see your things causes you untold stress. Or maybe you desire minimalism because you're eco-minded.

Help to broaden each other's perspective Discovering a new interiors style and a new way of organising can be seen as something you haven't yet tried. A maximalist could encourage a minimalist to broaden their colour palette while the minimalist could gently suggest ways the maximalist can shed 'just in case' items.

Be a maximalist within minimalist rules Many maximalists will have more than one version of something – for example, different sets of plates, jugs and cushions. Rather than having everything in circulation at once, rotate them. This way you get the benefit of owning beautiful things without sending the minimalist in your life to an early grave!

Can't compromise? This is the point at which you might want to 'zone' areas or dedicate spaces to either maximalism or minimalism, room by room.

Using colour to tidy

Neutral tones do go together, but there is also great pleasure to be had in organising by colour. Professional organisers and specialists in productivity often use it when formulating systems that are easy to implement and maintain.

Using colour to put things in order is almost like organising without even knowing you're doing it. How's that for making tidying fun! Here are a few suggestions for how to tidy using all the colours of the rainbow.

Books

Libraries may store books according to the Dewey Decimal System but there's nothing that says you have to do the same. There

Colour coding

Assign each child a colour in your home and use this for all their essential items including toothbrush, towel, laundry bin and storage box in the hallway. That way they will always know what's theirs – and you'll always know who has forgotten to pick up their towel!

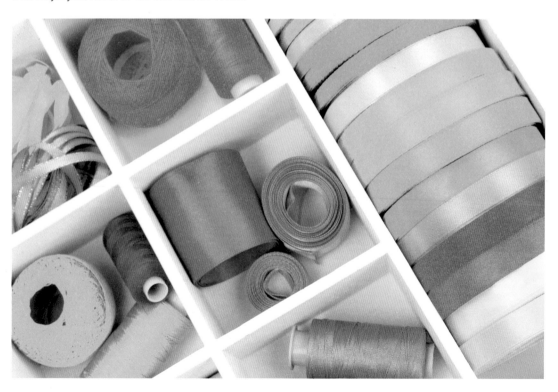

are a range of ways you can stow books away, from genre and author through to alphabetical order and – of course – colour order. Many people know their books by the colour of the covers so if you're one of these people, finding a volume within a rainbow of titles will be effortless. If you want more order but are still keen on a colour theme, batch books together by genre (e.g. travel) then colour theme them within that.

Clothes

There are different ways you can store your clothes including function (for example, all t-shirts and vests in one drawer) but there's nothing more fun than ordering them by colour. This not only gives you a 'heart soar' moment when you open your cupboard doors, it also enables you to quickly team clothes with each other according to colour. A rainbow effect takes away visual confusion and streamlines the decision process. Another colour tip for clothing is to colour-code hangers so that, for example, work outfits are on red hangers, leisure clothes on yellow hangers and evening wear on green hangers.

Crafting

Many of the materials we use for craft and art projects, such as paper, pens, fabrics and yarns, are things of great beauty in themselves so it seems a shame to stow them away where they can't be seen. Store them creatively, putting coloured pens in pots according to colour and piling fabric

swatches on open shelves so they can inspire you for your next project.

Home office and stationery

A straightforward way to organise your filing with colour is to choose a colour that corresponds to each category, such as hot pink for finance, yellow for household bills, light blue for insurance and red for personal. You could assign a colour for each of these in a suspension file system, simply changing the tab colour according to your needs (light blue may have more than one hanging file if you're including home insurance, car insurance, pet insurance and travel insurance, for example). Home office supply shops are full of colourful files, dividers, notepads and other equipment to make it easy for you.

Life tidying

When we think of tidying up our lives, we focus on the tangible, physical things – the spaces we occupy and the objects within them. But what about friendships and relationships? If we're ordering and space-clearing, life-tidying should be on the list, too.

Have you ever sat in a room that's a bit chaotic, but not cared because you're happy? Conversely, has emotional turbulence in a relationship or friendship, or in your work life, meant that all you can think about is internal chaos, no matter how ordered your surroundings? Humans are social creatures and the relationships we have – from partners, friendships and family relationships through to colleagues and aquaintances – really do matter. Good relationships and positive scenarios nourish us. While you are addressing practical tidiness in your physical space, why not think about tidiness in relation to your emotional space, too, and what areas you might need to tidy, life-wise.

What areas of life do you need to tidy?

There are all kinds of relationships and situations that might benefit from life-tidying, from improving the important and close ones through to purging the more toxic and superfluous. It is good to take a step back, and gain more clarity about what areas of your life could benefit from a tidy-up. Making changes is about a mind-shift and the right action will flow naturally from that.

Be with people who make you feel good

Take the time and make the effort to be with those who make you feel loved, calm and inspired. These may be old friends and contacts or new ones you've discovered by taking part in a new-found skill or hobby. Fulfilment in this way will also help to fortify you when it comes to areas of your life you can't easily change (like dealing with close but difficult relatives, perhaps). Ask yourself, does someone fill your heart with light or does it feel like they're dampening you down? Try to spend your time with people who are 'radiators' not 'drains', giving warmth and not taking energy.

Be brave and explain

Personal growth happens when we learn from our mistakes. If a friend or relative has become challenging, let them know (in a constructive way) or consider what changes can be made. Remember too that self-awareness and honesty works both ways, are you a support or a drain to other people? Life tidying doesn't always mean ending friendships and relationships. We have different friends for different things – the question is, is it a nourishing relationship?

Establishing boundaries can help to reframe relationships that have lost their way or got into an unacceptable groove, and to assess if it's time for some positive changes.

Tidying your work life

Feeling happy and fulfilled rather than unhappy and frazzled in the workplace is an important part of life tidying. Working out how to rationalise your time at work may mean getting the job done more quickly and efficiently. If you're going to be spending long hours at your desk, it is important to have a good space. This isn't just about whether your workspace is tidy; take time to assess whether your chair is comfortable enough,

your keyboard is ergonomic and you have a support stand for your laptop. If you feel you've got into bad work habits, find it hard to say no, and aren't good at discussing issues such as money, don't be afraid to enlist external help. A business coach can help you to prioritise and address key issues.

Time to self-nourish

Tidying your life is also about filling it with joy and fun. Look after your heart and soul by keeping a diary to reconnect with the joy of your own life story, creating music playlists to spark happiness, and set aside time each day to do something that is purely for you – even if it's only 15 minutes.

GETTING
READY TO
Tidy

Common barriers to tidying

There are all kinds of reasons why we can't get tidy. Some might call them 'excuses' but we call them 'barriers' instead: keeping tidy is hard enough without negative value judgements getting in the way of progress.

Many of us do want to be tidier – statistics show that 80 per cent of us think it's important to keep our homes in some kind of order. However, 75 per cent of us feel that accomplishing this is a hassle. There's no doubt about it, achieving some kind of order can feel like a massive mountain to climb, even a whole range of mountains. While the desire to be tidy and the ability to achieve it seems to come naturally to some people, for many of us it feels tricky at the least or impossible at the worst. As we discovered

earlier in this book, both science and psychology can be major obstacles to us getting things into some kind of organisation and order. But there are other reasons or barriers that can stand in the way, too. The definition of a barrier is 'anything used or acting to block someone from going somewhere or from doing something', or simply 'to block something from happening'. Barriers can be very effective at blocking your hopes of a tidier life before they become reality! Some are practical (such as not

wanting to be wasteful by throwing items away) while others are more emotional (such as feeling like it's too big a job to cope with). And as we shall discover, whether you're a minimalist or a maximalist will impact what your vision of organisation and order actually is. Don't feel bad if these barriers sound only too familiar to you – they are facts of life we all deal with, to a lesser or greater degree.

As soon as you understand that these barriers to keeping tidy constantly infiltrate our lives, you'll hopefully also appreciate the importance of being kind to yourself. Being vexed will only add to your self-irritation (or irritation with others, if they are your tidiness barriers) and will stop you approaching the task of tidying with clarity and composure. Being compassionate towards yourself – not to mention others who may be helping you

– will help you make better decisions about what's staying and what's going.

Over the next pages, we'll be looking at some of the most common barriers to tidying that can get in the way of our best intentions, and how we can try to overcome them.

What is holding me back?

- Nostalgia
- The Three Ps: Pessimism, Perfectionism and Procrastination
- Temporary untidiness 'blips'
- Living in smaller spaces
- More stuff than ever before
- The war against waste
- Other people
- Communications clutter

Pessimism, Perfectionism and Procrastination

Do you have plans of tidying, only to find yourself putting it off? Maybe you assess the task and think, 'I'll never get everything sorted so I may as well not bother.' Or perhaps you're still waiting for the perfect time to get tidy.

If you intend to start tidying yet it never seems to happen, you could be suffering from the Three Ps: Procrastination, Perfectionism and Pessimism. They are often related or overlapping concepts, but all are capable of driving a wedge through our best plans to get order and organisation in our homes.

Perfectionism

This is another reason for procrastination. Perfectionists find it more psychologically acceptable to never tackle a task such as tidying up than to fail at it or fall short on standards or performance.

Pessimism

If you've procrastinated for long enough, possibly because you're worried you won't do it well or complete the task, you may end up feeling negative about even starting.

A 2011 study showed that perfectionists are more likely to be worriers and suffer from anxiety and depression.

Procrastination

We put things off for a variety of reasons, often because we don't really want to do them and would rather do something (read 'anything') else. Experts say reasons for procrastinating include ignorance, not having the skills, apathy, fixed habits, inertia, poor memory, physical problems and 'appropriate' delays. These may feel a bit like holding a mirror up to aspects of yourself you're not happy about, but don't feel bad – they're extremely common and they can definitely be worked with.

Do you find yourself saying:

'I don't even know where to start!'
'I don't want to start if I can't do all of it.'
'I'll do it after Christmas/in the holidays/when the kids leave home.'
'Tidying won't make the slightest bit of difference here.'
'I didn't know I was supposed to do that.'
'I don't know how to do it.'
'I really don't want to do this.'
'It doesn't make any difference if I put it off.'
'No one really cares whether I do this or not.'
'I need to be in the mood. I'm not.'
'I've always done it this way.'
'I work better under pressure.'

'I just can't seem to get started.'
'I just forgot.'
'I couldn't do it; I was unwell.'
'I'm just waiting for the best time to do it.'
'I need time to think this through.'
'This other opportunity will never come again, so I can't pass it up.'
There are masses of other potential excuses to exemplify how easy it is to put off tidying!

How tidying can help

Tackling the Three Ps – whether it's one or all of them – will help you take action in your quest for order. All of the Ps cause inertia. If you have a problem with any or all three of the Ps, you may benefit from the following:

• Use a timer to schedule in short periods of tidying focus.

• Avoid external interruptions such as your mobile or cellphone. Put it in another room, put it on silent, or switch it off.

• Break tasks into smaller, more manageable chunks. Gretchen Rubin, author of *The Happiness Project*, says, 'Don't let the perfect be the enemy of the good. Lower the bar. Actually spending ten minutes clearing off one shelf is better than fantasising about a weekend cleaning out the basement.'

• Tell a friend about your intentions.

• Give yourself a reward. Say to yourself 'If I finish tidying this cupboard out, I can visit my neighbour for a coffee for half an hour.'

• Do what you can. Confucius said, 'Better a diamond with a flaw than a pebble without.' Some tidying is definitely better than nothing.

Temporary untidiness 'blips'

You know how it is – life is bumbling along quite uneventfully when something happens to throw a spanner in the works. Whether it's good or bad, big or small, changes in your life can derail even the best tidiness plans.

Remember what John Lennon once said about life being the thing that happens when you're making other plans? With the best will in the world, even the most well-oiled tidiness machine can start grinding to a halt if something untoward or unexpected happens in our lives. Adverse life events such as divorce, illness or death can wreak havoc. Even the joyous birth of a baby or the arrival of a new pet can throw the most orderly home into disarray. Why? Because a change in routine and the status quo means that priorities inevitably realign and what was important yesterday – such as keeping the kitchen surfaces clutter-free – suddenly drops to the bottom of the list. When our lives are rattled or even turned upside down, all sorts of emotions come into play, too, such as shock, hopelessness and feeling overwhelmed, and these can bring inertia and creeping chaos with them.

Do you find yourself saying:
'It's normally really tidy in here. This isn't like me at all!'
'How can a puppy cause such mayhem?!'

Common stresspoints

As well as expected stressors such as divorce, death of a loved one or major injury, there are others on the Holmes and Rahe scale that may not even occur to you as stressful. These are just as capable of preventing tidiness as the bigger stressors. Here are just a few common untidiness 'blips'; when you come across them, expect some disruption – and be kind to yourself.

- Pregnancy.
- Retirement from work.
- Changing to a different line of work.
- Child leaving home.
- In-law troubles.
- Major change in financial state (including an improvement).
- Child changing to a new school.
- Major change in sleeping habits (getting more or less than usual).
- A holiday (big or small).
- Minor law violations (including parking tickets).
- Major change in the health or behaviour of a family member.
- Change in living conditions (including new home or renovation).

'I'm not feeling 100 per cent so tidying up just isn't a priority.'
'I wish I'd got more organised before the baby arrived…'
'My whole world has changed; tidying is the last thing on my mind.'

How tidying can help

Unknown impediments to order such as a death bring their own tidiness challenges because their unexpected and shocking nature can lead to such a life change in routine. In 1967, Holmes and Rahe developed a questionnaire called the Social Readjustment Rating Scale (SRRS) for identifying 43 major stressful life events. Major life changes such as a new job or retirement are on there but also even things like holidays because, lovely though they may be, they are a change in the usual routine (think of how all those piles of post-holiday washing mess the house up like nothing else!).

If there are known 'blips' on the horizon, like having a new baby or a child changing school, then getting a new system of organisation and order together beforehand can be one less thing to stress about.

Even if there aren't anticipated blips, life happens, and if you already have a system then anything unexpected should hopefully be easier to navigate through. You can focus on the emergency rather than worrying about disorder that may well add to your tension levels, not to mention not being able to find what you need when you need it.

More stuff than ever before

Do you find that as each year goes by you acquire more clothes, knick-knacks and books, despite wondering where you're going to store them? Are these new additions to your household standing in the way of you being tidy?

When you cast an eye around your home, do you spot objects you hardly ever use – maybe even some you've never actually used? You're not alone. Professor Danny Dorling of Oxford University says we have six times more stuff than the generation before us. The average person clings on to 32 unused items. However, this doesn't stop us accumulating more; we simply carry on buying and put unused objects into storage instead (the amount of self-storage space in the UK has doubled in a decade). Just 23 per cent of people who use self-storage visit them weekly and for the rest of us it's far less frequent. Not only are we wasting money to keep possessions we don't need, we're also managing to live perfectly well without them.

The keyring study

In a 2009 study, researchers gave 62 people with OCD keyrings, and asked them to rate their attachment on receipt of the gift and again a week later. Those who tended to hoard more were attached to the keyring immediately. This 'love at first sight' was also observed when hoarders went shopping.

Do you find yourself saying:

'I might need it someday so better keep it.'
'It'll be great for when we move to a bigger place.'
'It's important paperwork so I mustn't bin it.'
'It's only £/$ a month to store it…'

How tidying can help

Good organisation at home means we can do a proper audit of what we actually own. We are then better able to judge what we want or need to keep and what we are happy to shed. This is the key to reducing the volume of possessions we own. If we don't know what we've got, then how are we to ever know what's going to make the cut? Paring things back may save us money

through not having to store stuff, buy duplicates or even move to a bigger place. Besides, do we really need it? A recent study by Havas Worldwide showed that half of us could live happily without most of the things that we own. Tidying up so you have less stuff may also be good for your mind. Research in 2011 found that when your environment is cluttered, the chaos restricts your ability to focus and limits your brain's ability to process information compared to an uncluttered and organised environment.

On the one hand, our absent objects may keep stuff from cluttering up our homes but they may also mean we accumulate other items in their absence instead of assessing what we've got. Self-storage becomes a spare room or shed we are unlikely to clear out. Tackling the tidy-up can help you think about why you're keeping so many things.

Extreme tidying, extreme chaos

Both collecting and tidying are normal human activities (it is estimated around 30 per cent of adults are collectors). However, sometimes both of these can become problematic and even extreme, resulting in the following:

Hoarding disorder Also known as compulsive hoarding, this is when a person either excessively acquires possessions or has difficulty discarding them, regardless of their actual value. This results in living spaces becoming cluttered to the point that their use or safety is compromised. In its severest form it can be an immense burden for sufferers, their loved ones and society. Hoarding disorder is recognised as a mental health condition by the World Health Organisation and affects 2–5 per cent of the population. In a modern development on the theme, a 2018 academic paper suggests that digital hoarding can also be a problem.

Chronic disorganisation This is where you yo-yo between extremes of getting organised and becoming overwhelmed with your things. The term was coined by Judith Kolberg, author of Conquering Chronic Disorganization, and describes people who live amid clutter including paper, boxes or bags stacked around the home. They also have problems with time management and often end up 'fire-fighting' rather than long-term planning.

OCD. People mistakenly think that OCD is linked to hoarding. While hoarding can be a symptom of OCD (for example when hoarding comes with a fear of harming others if 'contaminated' belongings are thrown away) hoarding has been shown to be independent from other psychiatric disorders. OCD sufferers typically experience intrusive thoughts, obsessions or repetitive behaviours whereas general hoarders don't.

Living in smaller spaces

How many times have you said to yourself, 'I could do with an extra room – or two…'? Do you find yourself shoehorning your possessions into storage that doesn't seem adequate? Small spaces are a common issue for tidiness.

Some of us may have the luxury of living with ample space, storage and room for growth if our circumstances change (like the arrival of a new baby or accommodating an elderly parent). However, statistics suggest that for most of us it's more a case of the 'tiny house trend'. Between one-quarter and one-third of us are dissatisfied with our space, and living in ever smaller homes.

Did you know?
A fifth of us live in rented accommodation and this is expected to rise to a quarter by the end of 2021.

Do you find yourself saying:

'Agh! If only I had more storage!'

'I'm running out of space.'

'There's no room for visitors.'

'I think we need to move to a bigger place.'

'I'll just put it in storage. It doesn't cost much…'

Small space hacks

- Back-of-the-door storage.
- Window seats with storage underneath.
- Wheeled storage.
- Vertical storage.
- Hanging wall storage (great for renters).
- Disappearing desk.
- Drawer inserts to 'double stack' possessions.

How tidying can help

It stands to reason that you need space if you're going to store your belongings. With accommodation more in demand than ever before – an increase in single household numbers is adding to this strain – we are all tussling for limited space. If this is our reality, accepting that the space is what we are working with and being tidy within those parameters will help us both spatially and psychologically. Also, as we've seen already, we're accumulating more possessions than ever, and so struggle to fit everything we own into the space that we have.

The war against waste

Another obstacle to our ability to get tidy and stay that way is overconsumption – and waste. We keep on buying like there's no tomorrow and yet don't want to get rid of things we already own.

Every year we waste food, use up trees and discard unwanted plastic. We buy clothes, wear them an average of seven times then throw them out (or leave them languishing in the wardrobe!). Our behaviour isn't only having a financial cost, it's harming our planet, too. Since the 3Rs – reduce, reuse, recycle – were introduced as a concept in the 1970s we have become increasingly aware of our impact on the environment, whether it's choosing not to buy fruit wrapped in plastic, trying not to overconsume by buying things we don't need or minimising how many documents we print out. Figures show there was a 235 per cent increase in household recycling in England between 2000 and 2010. We still have some way to go – only nine per cent of the world's plastic is currently recycled – and many of us are also worried about waste. How does this relate to tidiness? Many of us don't want to throw things out unless we really have good reason to, because we feel it's wasteful and things should survive to see another useful day.

Do you find yourself saying:

'I've just bought a whole new summer wardrobe for £100! So cheap!'
'I'm drowning in plastic!'
'I hate to think how much food I waste…'

3R facts

Globally, more than 40 per cent of plastic is used just once, yet plastic can take 500 years to decompose.

Between 13 and 25kg of electrical and electronic equipment such as fridges and computers are thrown out per person per year. Think about giving these items instead to associations that will take on the job of restoring or refurbishing them.

Reduce Reuse Recycle

While our space is disordered and in need of organising, it's easy to fall into poor 3R habits, whether it's not knowing what's lurking in the back of your fridge, using plastic carrier bags instead of a 'forever' shopper, or buying brand-new clothes instead of heading to a charity shop.

Tidying will help you better understand your 3Rs and develop strategies and systems for every room. For example, by tidying your bathroom or utility room, you'll

create space to store bulk purchases such as recycled toilet paper (packaging represents 23 per cent of the weight of our household waste). In the following pages we give you some room-by-room ideas to help with tidying that will also benefit the environment. Not only will these tips help you to be more eco-friendly and save you money, they will also help in your quest for tidiness and order. Being environmentally-savvy means you'll run a much leaner and efficient household.

Bathroom

- Choose products made from recycled materials (such as recycled paper or bamboo toilet roll) or sustainable materials (such as bamboo toothbrushes).
- Buy products with recyclable packaging.
- Rather than bottled toiletries, use bars such as soap, shampoo or conditioner or choose eco-refillable bottles.
- Ditch the baby wipes and choose reusable cloths with water or mild soap instead.
- Babies use more than 4000 nappies or diapers before they're potty-trained. Help to reduce this burden on landfill by using real washable fabric nappies.

Utility room

- Use washable cloths instead of kitchen roll where you can, and buy recycled or sustainable varieties of paper.
- Buy concentrated products or refillable ones, such as detergents, fabric softeners and cleaners.
- Instead of buying a large range of different cleaning products named individually for a variety of surfaces and functions, choose a multi-purpose one.

Kitchen

• Buy in quantities adapted to what you need. Bulk-buying may seem economical but if you end up wasting it because it goes bad, it's not good for the environment, or your wallet. On the other hand, it is better to avoid buying mini portions of food sold in pouches and packets, which are high in packaging and cost more.

• Choose items packaged in cans and glass rather than non-recyclable plastics.

• Make the most of your freezer.

• Consider a doorstep delivery service for milk, organic vegetables and other fresh produce – the packaging is usually minimal and often returnable/reusable.

• Put products with a short use-by date at the front of your fridge or cupboard to remind you to use them first.

• Take shopping home in a 'bag for life' or a crate. Keep a folded-up tote or for-life bag with you for ad-hoc shopping.

• Re-use carrier bags as liners for small bins.

• Avoid single-use plastic products such as straws, cocktail stirrers, cups and plates, and use paper ones instead. Metal straws are a great eco option too.

• Put packed lunches in a reusable container rather than wrapped in cling film or foil.

Kids' spaces

• Reuse items wherever possible. Use scrap paper for drawing (on both sides, ideally) and re-use plastic tubs for felt-tips, pencils and crafting materials such as stickers and glitter.

• Make your own presents, cards and wrapping paper (e.g. a roll of lining paper with potato print decoration goes a long way and is great fun to do).

• When buying toys, choose products that use mains power, not batteries. This is a greener choice that will also reduce the need to store and dispose of batteries. Use rechargeable batteries where possible.

• Try out a local toy library instead of buying, so you can rotate and try out games without needing to keep and store them.

• Borrow equipment your baby is likely to grow out of, including clothing or furniture such as cots or changing tables, or buy them second-hand. Give them away again when you're done.

• Organising kids' birthday events? Avoid giving gifts with too much packaging and wrap them in recycled wrapping paper. Make invitations paperless and don't waste resources on party bags (just say 'no' to pointless plastic presents).

Home office

• Reduce paperwork by opting for paperless bank statements and bills.

• Reduce unsolicited mail by registering with a mail preference service and returning unwanted mail to the sender.

• If you're buying a computer, ask whether it can be easily upgraded so you buy new components when the time comes rather than a completely new computer.

• Buy refillable items such as printer cartridges and glue, and reuse folders and files rather than ordering new ones.

• Use scrap paper for notes and messages and use adhesive putty (such as Blu Tac) which can be reused time and again.

• Buy a solar-powered calculator or clock.

• Use rechargeable batteries in appliances rather than disposable ones.

• Swap magazines and periodicals with friends before giving yours away.

Garden

• Compost your garden and kitchen waste; if you don't have space for your own compost bin (or a garden) then many councils collect.

• Kill off weeds by covering them with old carpets, newspapers, and lawn mowings to save on weedkillers.

• Recycle plastic water bottles by cutting them down to seedling 'greenhouses'.

• Reuse household water on your plants.

• Dry clothes on a washing line outside rather than using a clothes dryer.

Other people!

Do you sometimes think, 'If I lived on my own I'd be so tidy'? As we saw in the chapter on 'The science of tidiness', things naturally tend towards disorder – and this is intensified when you add other humans into the mix.

Humans are social creatures. We love having people around us. However, there's no doubt about it – whether it's spouses, flatmates or children, other people can be a real hindrance when it comes to keeping tidy, and we know it!

It's been scientifically proven that living with other people can give us happier and longer lives. However, sharing your space can add other issues into the mix, including the thorny matter of tidiness. Statistics show that keeping things organised and tidy can be one of the things couples argue most regularly about. Children being messy is a reason for falling out, too. In fact, after not eating what's on their plates, or doing homework, an untidy bedroom is a top reason parents argue with their children.

But it isn't just people we live with who can hinder our tidiness plans. Visitors bringing gifts (lovely but do you need any more things?) and relatives passing on heirlooms are just a few ways that 'object creep' can start to spoil even the most streamlined system.

A word of caution: you can't always blame other people for untidiness, even if they are messing up your space. It is ultimately your responsibility to get things tidy, then to

'Cleaning your house while your kids are still growing is like shovelling the walk before it stops snowing.'

PHYLLIS DILLER

create a system and to let people know what that system is so they can comply. In other words, it's important to have ownership of your untidiness.

Do you find yourself saying:
'What did your last slave die of?!'
'Just put it into the washing basket, not on the floor!'
'I was given it as a gift by a friend, I can't get rid of it!'

How tidying can help
Getting other people involved in your tidiness goals can help to reduce the angst of the task. In fact, it's essential. Whoever you are sharing your space with has to be a willing adopter of any tidiness system you put in place or at the very least have a system that fits in with yours. Agree on a system

together, such as having a dedicated shelf or caddy for each person in the bathroom. You could create a 'messy box': if you're forever finding odd items around communal areas, have a box that you agree you'll all put things in, to be repatriated to where they belong.

You'll be doing kids a favour if you instil tidiness principles into them from an early age. They won't always live with you and being able to keep things in some kind of order will stand them in good stead for being flatmates, partners and even parents themselves. Tidying up and getting order in your home will also help you to make better decisions when a relative next says, 'I thought you might like Aunt Mary's silverplate tea set'. If you know that something doesn't fit into your system, both physically and emotionally, then it will be easier to say 'no'.

Hurdles of shared living

• Flatmates often keep different schedules so although they live together, they don't necessarily see each other that much. Schedule a day and a time when you're both or all free to tackle the untidy spots in your home. Working as a team will help you to get the job done quicker and will also help you to bond.

• If you have different views of what is tidy, talk about it – and be prepared to compromise. Living with someone who is messy can be challenging if you're neat and tidy. However, living with someone who nags about keeping tidy isn't much fun, either.

Virtual clutter

Are you as overwhelmed by information as you are by your possessions? Do you feel that even though you've just whipped a room into shape there's still virtual clutter weighing you down? This feeling is increasingly common.

When we talk about clutter, most of us think of physical things, like boxes, paperwork and piles of shoes. But virtual clutter is also becoming an increasing challenge when it comes to keeping our lives ordered and organised. Whether it's emails, computer files, photographs, eBooks or music files, as each day goes by we gather more and more data, all of which is in danger of distracting us and taking us one step further away from virtual tidiness. Each day, the average person receives 121 emails and sends 40 – way more messages than we ever received or sent when post arrived physically. However, almost half of these are spam and it is estimated we only open one-third of emails we receive. It's not just our email accounts that are putting us under pressure: the average person had seven social media accounts in 2018 compared to just three in 2012. No wonder virtual clutter feels like it's getting the better of us.

Do you find yourself saying:

'I have 20,000 unopened emails. I just ignore them.'
'I have so many apps on my phone.'
'I know they messaged me, I just can't remember on what platform.'

How tidying can help

New research suggests that virtual clutter can make us feel as overwhelmed and tense as physical clutter. As with physical tidying, a virtual clear-up may help to reduce our stress levels. A touch of virtual clutter management may also help to make us more productive. Receiving too many unecessary emails is stopping many of us from getting our real work done.

Virtual tidiness tips

Tidy up your computer Your computer should be working for you, not adding an extra layer of stress to your life. Organise your local files, clear your desktop (it's the first thing you see when you power up), consider cloud storage, get an external hard drive and delete apps you don't use.

Remember the 800:20 email rule Graham Allcott, author of *How to be a Productivity Ninja*, says that most emails are 'just noise' and of around 800 emails received only 20 will truly matter. Don't feel guilty if you find yourself deleting hundreds of emails. Many of them aren't worth reading and certainly don't need to be kept once read.

Allocate tidy-up time to your emails Set aside regular time to tackle emails. How often you

do this will depend on what you do for a living; it could be anything from a few minutes each hour to a half hour blitz every day. This will help you feel like you're keeping on top of your email account. Don't forget to manage spam or junk mail by making sure you unsubscribe to unwanted messages and consign them to the junk folder.

But, don't get fixated on zero Many of us have thousands – if not tens of thousands – of unopened emails in our accounts (on average we only open only a fraction of our emails). According to Merlin Mann, who coined the 'Inbox Zero' phrase in 2007, we should be regularly dealing with this digital admin until the number is zero. However, another school of thought describes the exercise as 'structured procrastination' along the lines of meticulous to-do lists. Professor of Psychology and Behavioral Economics Dan Ariely says sorting emails tends to take precedence over the things that are important to us. Don't get obsessed with getting it down to zero – your life won't be any better for it.

Use a password app An app such as 1Password will provide you with the security of selecting unique passwords to protect all your online accounts without having to remember them and store them separately.

In praise of 'stuff'

It might seem contradictory in a book about tidying and space-clearing to offer a countering viewpoint, but it is worth remembering that not all possessions are lacking in personal value and pleasure, and that there is a place for them too.

Earlier in the book we've talked about how having too many objects around us may cause confusion and stress. We're constantly being told to purge and to only keep things that give us joy. Even the dictionary description of 'clutter' – to 'cover or fill (something) with an untidy collection of things' – is embedded with negativity, conjuring up an impression of overwhelming chaos and implying it's bad to venerate 'stuff'.

But could it be that we do derive pleasure from being surrounded by many of our things and shouldn't necessarily be in such a hurry to get rid of them? Should we always streamline our lives and rush headlong towards a perceived ideal of clear surfaces and pared-back minimalism? In *The Joy of Leaving Your Sh*t All Over The Place*, Jennifer McCartney talks about FABpers (Fatally Addicted to purging your Belongings) and says that rather than being liberating, being a FABper is actually the opposite of being free. She says we're in danger of thinking there's something wrong with us if we want things and aren't particularly worried about where they go.

Some tidiness experts, including Marie Kondo, have suggested that by keeping hold of a multitude of possessions we are clinging on to the past. But is this really the case? And if we do have lots of objects that give us joy, why are we rushing to shed them? Maybe the time has come to also celebrate keeping hold of 'clutter' rather than being made to feel that its ownership is a character weakness that makes us morally inferior to people who choose to have little around them. After all, the things we own have often shaped who we are today, whether they are souvenirs, books, CDs, records or anything else. Possessions can have memories embedded in them that remind us of our humanity, from the very best of times to the most poignant.

We need an attitude shift towards our possessions, seeing them as things to love, cherish and adore. We should be free to display them with impunity without someone constantly suggesting we should be streamlining in order to travel 'lighter'

'I want to lead the Victorian life, surrounded by exquisite clutter.'

FREDDIE MERCURY

through life. None of us is in a position to take our possessions with us when we die so why shouldn't we just enjoy them while we have the capacity to do so? Rather than stopping us being who we want to be, the experience of loving your clutter can be mindful and focussed on the present, helping you to be happy with who you are right now.

So, how do we reconcile clutter with clearing? Look around your home and make a note of what it is that makes you happy about the space. If a cluster of ceramic objects is making your heart sink, then a purge is what your personality is probably urging you to do. However, if the collection makes your heart soar – and you're secretly thinking, 'I'd really like to expand this collection…' – chances are you're a creative and a lover of 'exquisite clutter' (to borrow Freddie Mercury's words). When it comes to tidying, you can still follow the principles in this book but understand that you'll probably have more items in your 'love' pile than other people. When it comes to storage options, you may want to look at ones that allow for decorative display such as display shelves or cupboards with glass doors. Handled in the right way, clutter doesn't have to be a dirty word: it can be a creative and stimulating way of life.

Managing nostalgia

Dealing with nostalgic items can be a tall order. Maybe they're representative of idyllic times, or a marker of poignant events gone by. Oliver James, psychologist and author of *Affluenza*, says our identity is increasingly associated with objects and throwing them away is tantamount to throwing part of ourselves away.

Have you ever kept hold of something simply because it's been part of your life and personal landscape for as long as you can remember? Maybe you don't even like it that much but can't bear to let it go. Research has found that 90 per cent of us are unable to part with such possessions. Why is it that nostalgia can hinder rational decision-making when we're trying to get tidy and organised? Psychology has explanations for this:

The endowment effect
This theory has been observed for thousands of years. Around 340BCE, Aristotle said: 'For most things are differently valued

by those who have them and by those who wish to get them: what belongs to us, and what we give away, always seems very precious to us.' This is the essence of the endowment effect: we value things more when we own them. Research even shows that we can have owned something for just a few minutes but get attached so quickly that we're even willing to pay to keep it. It's the process of getting our hands on something that causes it to appear special.

Loss aversion
This concept is related to the endowment effect in the sense that once we own an item, surrendering it feels like loss, and this feels uncomfortable because humans are essentially loss-averse. We aren't happy about losing what we own, even if we're choosing to get rid of it (it has been said that 'losses loom larger than gains') and it is thought that the pain of losing is psychologically twice as powerful as the pleasure of gaining. Loss aversion also means we tend to stick with what we've already got, unless there's a good reason or incentive to change. Keeping hold of objects effectively prevents us from feeling loss.

The comfort of the past

Some experts believe that extreme nostalgia can hold us back, interfering with our attempts to cope with present circumstances. However, others say that nostalgia can be a highly positive thing. Reminiscing about the past promotes happiness and boosts feelings of social connectedness. We also know from studies that when we think about the past, although we might like to pop back and visit it, the majority of us don't want to stay there – we're just after the best bits. Keeping hold of nostalgic objects can help us to achieve this balance: living in the present with a nod to the past, and an acknowledgement that those powerful memories can be strongly intertwined with who we are.

As psychology professor Constantine Sedikides puts it, nostalgia is 'the perfect internal politician, connecting the past with the present, pointing optimistically to the future'. Nonetheless, although it may give us a warm fuzzy feeling, nostalgia may also render us less discerning when it comes to auditing our personal 'things', and less capable emotionally of keeping them in some kind of order.

Do you find yourself saying:

'It cost me a lot of money.'
'My grandma left it to me.'
'I wouldn't even know where to start!'
'Sorting things out stresses me out.'
'I might need it one day.'
'I'm saving it for my grandchilden.'

Memory game

Do you remember the 'tray game' when you were a kid, where you had to try and memorise objects when they were no longer in sight? Make a list of your most valued possessions from memory. If you can't remember you own something without a visual prompt, it doesn't mean you don't need it but it may well be an indication that it matters less to you than you realise.

How tidying can help

Few of us have the room – or the desire – to keep everything from our past. However, by creating a system of order and organisation, we'll be able to understand more fully what would be psychologically nourishing for us to keep. If we are surrounded by items from our past (or from other people's) it may be taking up both physical and emotional space that could be occupied by the here and now. Equally, treasured pieces we do decide to keep will be better showcased if they're not drowning amidst 'So what?' objects. Nostalgia can stop us passing things on or throwing them away, even if they don't fit in our homes (space- or taste-wise) and are of no use to us. Tidying is so much more than just a physical process – it can also be emotionally draining, especially if you're sorting through photos, letters or a relative's belongings after they've gone. So how can we do it?

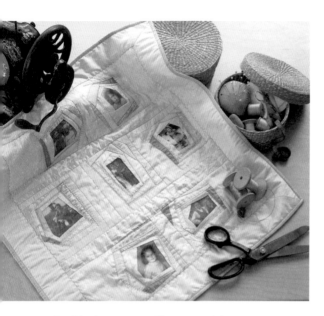

Be kind to yourself as you tidy

Feeling strong emotions such as sadness or melancholy are normal so pace yourself, for your heart and soul.

Connection to the past doesn't mean you're living in the past Some people suggest that keeping objects from our past (or, indeed, from before we even existed) keeps us from living in the present and looking to the future. This isn't necessarily the case: seeing objects as a point of connection can be a joyful thing. Not all retrospective moments are filled with longing. For example, a jarful of shells from a childhood holiday may kindle the happiest memories with no melancholy.

See yourself as a custodian of objects Ever heard the saying, 'A hearse doesn't have a trailer'? Whatever you own, you can't take it with you so while you're living, exalt in having things that bring you joy. See yourself as a custodian of objects – looking after them while they are with you before they belong to someone else one day. Taking pleasure in this temporary ownership can help to free you up from feeling bad about the potential weight of possessing things.

Understand that your memories are intrinsic, not extrinsic It's easy to look at an object and not only think that the memory is embedded within it but that without it that memory will fade. But wait – we still recall things from when we were at school or a relative who has long gone, without them being in front of us. Our memories are encoded somewhere deep within our brains and, for the large part, do a great job of staying. Our memories are in our mind and the object merely triggers them.

Honour special objects before you say farewell to them If you're keeping them, keep them safe in a memory box. If not, take photographs of sentimental items before you send them on their way. This is a simple way of 'keeping' the object as a visual prompt rather than being weighed down by it (emotionally, physically or both). Before you pass an object on, whether it's to a relative,

Keeping a record

Make a note of what each object is as you put it in the memory box so you know exactly when and what they relate to. You may think you'll never forget something but give it another ten years and you might!

friend or a charity shop, pause to reflect what it has meant to you in your life, take a photo of it – or use it one last time, if you like – then thank it for its service. It has been a good friend but it's time for it to move on.

Repurpose heirlooms

In her book *The Joy of Less*, Francine Jay says that heirlooms alone 'can paralyze our decluttering'. Sometimes we acquire objects that we can only envisage in their original iteration and that can stop us from enjoying them in the present. As a result, we end up not using them but also not being able to get rid of them. They are effectively stuck in a no-man's land. Repurposing them will help you to interact with them differently, enabling you to integrate them positively into your life in the here and now. For example, use the teacups from an old tea service to put plants in, or repurpose the fabric from a wedding or special dress.

Create a memory box

Memory or keepsake boxes are a good way of celebrating favourite meaningful objects and keeping them for posterity. Choose a largish plastic box with a lid so it can evade damage, wherever it is stored (it might end up in a damp garage). Other options include a decorative box or suitcase (Meminio do beautiful leather keepsake suitcases with matching folders and books). Every member of your household should have a box each – even young children (start the habit young!). Bear in mind the space you have

Create a memory bunny

If you or your children have treasured items of clothing, a muslin cloth or an old 'sucky' blanket you'd like to keep, why not immortalise it through crafting? There are companies on Etsy that will make memory bunnies from fabric you send through to them, or you can find a pattern there to make your own. Or how about a patchwork cushion?

and perhaps look through the box once a year (choose a memorable date such a birthday) so you can curate what stays and what goes.

Memory box suggestions

• Postcards and greetings cards from key people in your life. You don't need to keep them all, just a representative sample.
• Letters. There's nothing more evocative than someone's handwriting.
• 'Firsts' such as first tooth, first lock of haircut hair, first shoes, first drawing or painting, first cuddly toy.
• Tickets to special events, such as the first concert you went to together.
• Records of important milestones, such as a child's baby book, diaries, school reports and (selected) school books.
• Certificates and important trophies.
• Holiday mementos.
• Aromas such as an old perfume bottle; specific smells can help us recall memories.

Storage solutions

There's no doubt about it – smart storage can be the difference between chaos and calm. Whatever room it's for, thinking about what you really need and why can help you create a tidiness system that you can stick to.

If you have possessions, you'll need somewhere to put them. Some experts say that clever storage solutions – like boxes, racks, units and stands – are the key. An organised space can not only look good and maximise your space but it can also create the illusion of making a small space seem larger. Some others are convinced that when we focus on storage solutions we are simply finding ways to keep hold of things we don't really need. Marie Kondo, author of *The Life-Changing Magic of Tidying Up*, says that 'Storage experts are hoarders'. There may be some truth in this, if things are stored and rarely seen or used. However, storage can be life-changing if it's fit for purpose. What is the 'right' storage? It's about choosing a

place that creates an intuitive home for something so it doesn't take great effort to put it away – or find it again.

Key storage considerations

Usability Those wicker baskets you've bought for the kitchen may look attractive now, but how will they fare after months of being coated with airborne grease? Or those piles of stacked containers look neat but how are you going to access the one at the bottom of the heap? Solutions need to be practical or you won't use them.

Visibility Transparent containers are good for being able to see your possessions (although you might also decide that is unattractive, depending on the contents). But knowing what you've stored where, quickly and simply, is important.

Accessibility Are your objects at the right height for you and others to access them easily and safely? If you or other members of your household use objects frequently they should be easy to get to. Keep lesser-used items in the more out-of-reach areas.

Types of storage

If you're a maximalist who likes displaying their objects and isn't planning on moving,

your storage needs will differ to a minimalist living in rented accommodation.

Fixed storage Twin slot shelving using fixed wall uprights means shelves can be moved around, useful if your storage requirements are likely to change. A more permanent solution is having bespoke furniture made; you can get exactly what you want, as well as maximising quirky spaces.

Movable storage This is useful if you are renting or are intending to move soon, or if you like to ring the changes and shift your furniture around. Ladder shelving that props up against a wall is an option, as are display shelves that hang from a peg or screw. Trollies are great if you have items you need to use in more than one place, perhaps for

kids' crafting projects or for outdoor cooking.

Storage for hiding We all have items we don't want to see regularly, such as cleaning products and occasional cooking utensils like slow-cookers and popcorn makers. As well as lesser-used cupboards for such purposes, it's worth thinking about storage to sit within these – for example, plastic storage boxes to organise oddments.

Storage for display As well as objects we want to hide away, we have those we want to show off. The past few years has seen the rise of the shelfie, where we are much more conscious of what we put on our shelves and how we arrange them. Think about storage solutions that have no doors so that nothing gets in the way of what you can see.

THE STAGES OF
Tidying

Stage 1: The tidying mindset

When you've got it in your mind that you have to tidy, it may be tempting to forge ahead without being properly prepared. However, as US President Benjamin Franklin said, 'By failing to prepare you are preparing to fail.'

The first of our four stages of tidying is about getting yourself into the right tidying mindset, before moving on to the second stage of practical preparation. Here's how to achieve this most effectively:

DON'T.....

Put it off or make excuses not to do it If it helps you, set a date to do it, write it in the diary and don't keep stalling. Set an alert on your phone or prime a friend to remind you. Whatever it takes.

Do it half-heartedly If you do, it will take longer and you may even stop part-way through (and find it hard to go back again). Remember, even 10, 20 or 30 minutes is a time during which you can meaningfully achieve something in (tidying out your stationery cupboard, for example). Be committed to the task but don't…

What are my tidiness goals

Now is the time to ask why you want to tidy. Spend up to half an hour really thinking about how you'd like your home to look and feel. Come up with a list of affirming statements and write them on a piece of card so you can keep on looking at them throughout each tidy.

- 'I'll be free of that sinking feeling when I walk through my front door.'
- 'I'll be able to invite friends round without feeling embarrassed.'

- 'My home will feel inviting, calm and full of possibilities.'
- 'I'll get rid of some emotional baggage by tidying and getting rid of things.'
- 'My head will feel clearer and I'll be able to find things.'
- 'I won't constantly be thinking of all the untidy areas nagging away at me!'
- 'I don't want to leave chaos (or embarrassing or awkward scenarios) for other people when I die.'

Strive for perfection Gretchen Rubin, author of *Happier At Home*, says: 'Don't let the perfect be the enemy of the good.' Just commit to starting and take the rough with the smooth. You'll fly through some parts while others may be a physical or emotional wrench. Go with it and don't stop because it doesn't feel good enough.

DO...

Focus on your goals to keep you on track While you may derive comfort from having your things around you, having an excess of things could be holding you back, both physically (such as redecorating or rededicating space) or mentally (stopping other projects from commencing, for example). Look at the 'What are your tidiness goals' box above to see if any of your tidiness goals could be met by a chuck-out.

Start to disengage from your possessions We spend our lives accumulating when in reality anything we own will only be ours for the duration of our lifetime. Start the mental process of letting go by acknowledging that it may be someone else's turn to own something of yours and be happy that you'll be spreading joy.

Be kind to yourself as you tidy Tidying can be an emotional process, to say the least. Expect to feel some turbulence as you sort, and expect to feel a bit tired. Take regular breaks, tidy with a friend and, if possible, give yourself some space between tidying tasks (a day or two, for example) to give yourself the chance to recharge batteries.

Talk to others about your tidiness goals Whether it's a friend who can help to motivate you or a group where you can be sure of a kind response, involving others can keep you on track, and your goals realistic.

Stage 2: Practical prepping

You've got yourself into the right mindset, now it's time to move to the next stage – preparation. Having what you need in the way of storage and labels all ready to hand is key to a smooth tidying-up session.

This stage is about gathering everything you physically need to get tidying, from pens and stickers through to a buddy to help you, if needed. It is simple advice but collating the basic kit before you start – as well as deciding what and when you're going to tidy – means you won't have to break off to find a pen or a roll of stickers. This also means it

will be less likely that your tidying mission will be derailed. Once you've got the tools together, you can start to put them to use.

Gather your tidying tools

Getting what you need for your tidy sounds like an obvious thing to do but if you're not prepared you could get five minutes into a

tidying session only to discover you need to make a trip to the shops for bin liners, costing you at least 30 minutes of tidying time. Some of these tips are practical, such as plastic boxes or bin liners, while others are motivators (a friend) or mood-boosters (music, drinks and snacks).

• Paper or card (to make category pages for sorting).
• Magic marker or Sharpie.
• Plastic boxes or crates (to go with your 'Sort it' cards).
• Sturdy bin liners.
• Cleaning products (for wiping surfaces or boxes).
• Sticky labels (including coloured dots for sorting possessions).
• Drinks and snacks for those all-important breaks.
• A timer.
• The help of a friend – if you like.
• Music or the radio, for company.

Consider your storage solutions

These are tidying tools in their own right. By storage solutions we mean bags, baskets, bins, boxes, drawers, hangers, organisers, racks, rails, shoe stackers, stands, units and trays. Look at the room you're planning to tidy and assess what storage solutions you need on a basic level – for example, do you need shoe boxes or a belt hanger for your bedroom tidy? In practice you may end up needing solutions you hadn't even realised you needed. This is fairly inevitable. The main

thing is you at least have some options to hand so you don't have to stop mid-tidying (or jettison it altogether) because you haven't thought about where objects you're planning to keep are actually going to live. We've made suggestions for room-appropriate storage solutions in each of the room by room sections in the next chapter.

Make 'Sort it' markers

Whether you're using boxes to put cleared objects into or simply using pieces of paper or card to demarcate areas on the floor, you'll need to write headings so you know where to place things as you sort. This is an important aspect of organised tidying and spending just a bit of time to create these will save you time in the long run. These are some typical marker headings, some of which overlap but which indicate the main decision about your item:

• Give away
• Recycle
• Dispose/throw away
• Keep
• Relocate
• File
• To be actioned
• Special objects

Give away

What goes here: Things you don't need any more but still feel some connection to. 'Give Away' includes anything you can gift to friends or give to charity (knowing it will go to a good home). This also includes objects that charities can recycle if they can't sell, such as old clothes.

What doesn't: Broken objects (charity shops won't be able to sell them and friends and loved ones won't thank you).

Recycle

What goes here: Anything that can be recycled, either by your roadside recycling service or at a recycling centre.

What doesn't: Things that have potential value

The 'not sure' pile

It's totally fine to also have a 'not sure' pile: being 'not sure' is human. A 2018 US study found that decision-making can be hard for humans, especially when there are more than 15 options available. The researchers found that we make the best decisions when we have fewer options (think of menu overload!). When you're tackling tidying, there will inevitably be objects that you just can't make a decision about, especially if you're surrounded by a bunch of things you've cleared from a cupboard or drawer. This is normal! See the 'not sure' pile as a place where you put objects that you genuinely torn about whether to keep or purge. Sometimes we need to keep things in a 'holding pattern' for a while until we can make a decision about their fate.

to a charity shop or conversely things that really ought to go in the bin (for example, if it's broken, threadbare or a pair of shoes you can only find one of). See the section on avoiding waste and the 3Rs on pages 40–43 for more suggestions, and the Resources address list at the back of the book.

Dispose/throw away

What goes here: Anything that's broken, empty or destined for the dump. Out-of-date cosmetics or anything that is worn out, broken or makes you say 'I'll get round to fixing it soon', as chances are you won't. (If there are things you will get mended, put them in the 'to be actioned' pile.)

What doesn't: Anything that still has life in it or can be reused, recycled or disposed in a green fashion (think computers, batteries, ink cartridges and electrical goods).

Keep

What goes here: This is for objects you still need in your life (including practical ones) as well as objects that lift your heart and make you feel good. This should be a 'feel good' pile of objects you really want or need.

What doesn't: 'Keep' isn't the place for objects that are broken, objects that still work but you don't like, or objects someone gave you that you can't give away because you feel guilty.

Relocate

What goes here: This is the category for objects that have very obviously migrated to the wrong room or that are going to be repurposed to live elsewhere in your home, such as make-up that's in the bathroom but is destined for your bedroom. This is also for objects to be stored in an attic or basement (first be ruthless: do you really need them?).

What doesn't: 'Relocate' isn't an opportunity to shunt things into another room where they'll languish without being sorted. It's the chance to repatriate objects or give them proper new homes.

File (paperwork)

We are constantly bombarded by paperwork such as utility bills, bank statements and instruction manuals, as well as items such as catalogues or sales brochures that we intend to look at when we have time. As a result, paper seems to continually creep into most rooms we tidy.

What goes here: Any paperwork you know you need to keep (see the Home Office section on pages 92–95). Also paperwork you want to keep, such as meaningful letters, cards and children's artwork.

What doesn't: Paperwork you know you can throw away. Keep a separate 'Shredding' pile and a wastepaper bin to hand to deal directly with these.

To be actioned

What goes here: Objects you need to deal with in some way. For example things to be returned to people or discussed before you dispose. Objects to be returned to shops or sold, and also items for repair or alteration.

Work with a buddy

Research shows that people who support each other to lose weight as part of a 'buddy' system lose more than those who don't – and keep it off. Try this with tidying and work with a 'buddy' – a relative or good friend – to help you commit to getting and staying organised. Choose someone who will help you to make good decisions with compassion and understanding – and who won't get distracted or go off on a tangent!

What doesn't: Items you won't get round to fixing or selling: be realistic and either 'Dispose' or 'Give away'. Paperwork to action doesn't go here either; these best belong in the 'File' pile with your other documents, though it is a good idea to create an 'action now' sub-box or folder.

Special objects

What goes here: Objects that are destined for your 'Memory Box' (see how to create one in the section about managing nostalgia on pages 50–53) and that tug at the heart-strings. Keep this pile away from the others so you're not tempted to sort it in the middle of tidying. Emotional objects are the great stealers of tidying time!

What doesn't: Anything that's in your 'Keep' pile that you're keeping because you love it but that isn't for the 'Memory Box' (perhaps because you still display or use it frequently).

Stage 3: Allocating time

How are you going to organise your tidying time? The next key stage of preparation is to plan a timetable to keep you focused and motivated. Here are examples of time allocations for you to work to.

The approach taken by this book is to tidy room by room so that you can focus on one place and the zones within it, depending on how much time you have to spare. However, whatever your chosen method it is good to work to a timetable so you feel you are in control and that the efforts don't feel open-ended (and never-ending).

Good timetables to work to are a full day, a half day and 'light bites' (smaller chunks of time). As you'll see, we've factored in time to clear up after your tidying sessions. Leaving things lying around may be a luxury (especially if you share your space with other people) but it can also be highly demotivating and end up causing more mess than you started with. Clearing up post-tidy is an aid to preventing chaos.

Decide how long you've got The time you have to spend will inform what space to tackle first. If you've got less than an hour, it's likely to be part of a room, but if you've got a day or a weekend, you can work on something bigger or a whole room.

Start with a room you're not emotionally connected to A room such as a bathroom, kitchen or utility room should be a more straightforward tidy because it's intensely practical.

Tidying timetables

Full day
9am to 11am – start sorting
15 minutes – coffee break
11.15am to 1.15pm – more sorting
45 minutes – lunch break
2pm to 4pm – more sorting
15 minutes – tea break
4.15pm to 5pm – clear up
5pm – stop what you are doing

Morning session
9 to 10.30am – start sorting
15 minutes – coffee break
10.45am to 12.15pm more sorting
15 mins – tea break
12.30pm to 1pm clear up
1pm – stop what you are doing

Afternoon session
1.30pm to 3pm – start sorting
15 minutes – tea break
3.15 to 4.45pm – more sorting
15 minutes – tea break
5pm to 6pm – clear up
6pm – stop what you are doing

Choose a 'tidying target' Your target could be big or small, general or specific ('I want to clear the top of my dressing table', for example). This will be dictated by how much time you're allocating or what you want to accomplish (is your plan to clear your make-up drawer or are you hoping to blitz an entire home?). Say that target out loud or write it down so you can keep reminding yourself, even if you get distracted.

Set your timer A good way to stick to your timetable is to set stages into your stopwatch or phone clock so they go off throughout the allocated time and keep you on track. If not, a kitchen timer will do.

Light bites

You may not have a whole or even a half day to tidy but you can still make good progress with 10-, 20- or 30-minute chunks. Decide how long you've got and where you want to tidy then set a timer to make sure you keep to it. That way you'll keep motivated and focused. Short bursts are ideal for a small area such as a shelf, nightstand or underwear drawer. The great thing about light bites is that you can fit them in when you have a few spare minutes that you'd otherwise idle away.

Try this:

If you are planning to tackle two rooms in a day, use the Morning and Afternoon timetables concurrently (one after the other) to help you apportion your time, rather than the Full Day.

Keystone habits

In his book *The Power of Habit*, Pulitzer-prizewinning author Charles Duhigg talks about the importance of 'keystone habits' – little changes that can lead to a cascade of other changes. He says that simply making your bed each day is correlated with better productivity, a greater sense of well-being and even 'stronger skills at sticking with a budget'. Duhigg explains it's because 'those initial shifts start chain reactions that help other good habits take hold'. The message here is, don't think that small amounts of tidying are pointless: they're not. Just doing something, making a start, will set you on the way.

Stage 4: Starting to tidy

You've got your mindset in the right place for tidying, the equipment needed to the ready, worked out the categories to sort your things into, and decided how long you've got. Now it's time to start, applying the principles you've learnt.

Start small – and set goals

Some people are put off by the thought of a major purge or Spring clean. Remember, you don't have to do everything at once. That's a commitment waiting to be broken. Choose a room then specific areas within that room, such as books, cosmetics, shoes or a shelf or desk. Starting with a small goal leads to a cascade of good keystone habits.

Take a photo of the space you're tidying A 'before' picture will enable you to see where you need to tidy. An 'after' photo will show you how far you've come, too.

It looks worse!

'You have to break an egg to make an omelette.' Tidying is a contrary entity – it generally necessitates things getting messed up before they take on a new, more ordered form. That's why having some kind of method to the process is really helpful, to stop things descending into chaos and overwhelm you, and potentially causing you to give up. Push through the discomfort of things looking temporarily messy (but do keep going). It'll be worth it.

Clear a space on the floor You'll need plenty of space for clearing so make an area on the floor for sorting. Before you start, move furniture items into another room if it's easy to do and they are getting in the way. Tell other home-dwellers what you're doing.

Create your 'Sort it' zones Put your 'Sort it' markers on the floor in front of you. Make them all accessible so you can easily allocate objects to them as you go (having them in a line or a semi-circle in front of you works well). Have boxes or bin liners to the ready.

Clear the decks as soon as you can Once you have sorted objects in the Give Away, Recycle or Dispose 'Sort it' zones, bag or box them up and set them aside so you can create more physical space and headspace for the next things to be sorted, and to differentiate clearly from items being kept.

It is important to try to clear up as you go along. The sooner you can move your allocated piles and boxes on to their intended final destination the better. If your tidying session ends with you circulating objects from one room to another, or stuffing them away in a box or basket without any planning or method, chances are the chaos will begin again.

'Do I really need it?' checklist

As you put things in your 'Sort it' zones, ask yourself these five cardinal questions. That way you can evaluate if it's a keeper – or destined for pastures new, whether this is a new room or a new life. Print these questions out as a prompt as you tidy:

• 'Do I use it often or have a real need for it?'
• 'Do I really love it and would I miss it if it was gone?'
• 'Do I own something similar and can do without this one?'
• 'Do I need to keep hold of it for official reasons?'
• 'How often do I use it and where does that happen (e.g. which room should it be in)?'

Where to start

Where you begin is up to you although for a Spring clean-type purge, we advise you to start with your least emotional rooms. This is so you don't get bogged down sorting such things as photographs, papers and baby clothes. It's hard to get reflective about a bath sponge or a bottle of face wash.

The time you take to tidy each room isn't prescriptive: it's likely that if you've got a large kitchen you're going to have to dedicate more time to it than if you've got a galley-style space. Equally, a small office may look like a diminutive space but if it's packed full of documents it might eat up a lot of your time. Just be aware of this as you tackle your specified rooms.

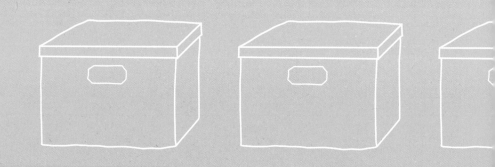

Tidying
ROOM BY ROOM

Bathroom

The bathroom or shower room is an ideal location to start tidying. Why? Because, by and large, this room is smaller and easier to tackle, and an inherently utilitarian space filled with easy-to-part-with possessions.

Even if it's a space you go to unwind, relax and reflect, a place to connect with your inner self, the objects a bathroom contains are likely to be functional rather than imbued with feeling and emotional connections; toiletries and make-up, cleaning products and towels rather than mementos and nostalgic objects. As a result, the process of tidying your bathroom – from chucking things out through to choosing the right storage for the objects you decide to keep – should be a straightforward one.

Quick tidy or big clear-up? Use the 'Allocating time' section (pages 64–65) to work out what amount of time you have, whether it's 10, 20 or 30 minutes, or something longer like a half-day or a full-day. This will help you manage your expectations.

Lay down your 'Sort it' cards This will help to keep you focused and enable you to start assigning items to specific categories from the outset.

Decide what storage you're going to need Bearing in mind how the room is going to be used, think what is most practical in the way of shelves, cupboards, cabinets and containers, and where they are best placed for convenient access. Where can you store things like towels, and spare toilet paper rolls? Some suggestions are given overleaf.

Clear out caddies and units Take everything off surfaces and empty the drawers and cupboards. Put everything in the middle of the floor with your 'Sort it' labels. If your bathroom floor isn't big enough for this, do the sorting in another room or even use the bath tub.

Throw away unwanted cosmetics and toiletries This could include dried-up or nearly-used up bottles you aren't going to finish in reality, and unopened items you don't like – perhaps these can regifted. Rinse out and recycle bottles and containers where possible.

Start populating your 'Sort it' piles. Are there any items that can be put in the 'Give away' pile? If they are still in-date, they could be repurposed as a school raffle prize or given away to charity.

'Do I really need it?' Keep referring to the five questions on page 67 to keep you on track when making decisions as you sort. Check the 'Bathroom giveaway list' for items you can safely blitz. Perhaps this is the time to lose all the third-best towels that you don't use. Think about how you can reduce, reuse or recycle these items.

Remove non-bathroom items When you've sorted the last object, remove anything from the room that isn't staying there. This includes cosmetics if you have decided to relocate them to another room such as a bedroom or dressing room.

Do you need additional storage solutions? Maybe you need more jars or an extra cosmetics tray or a big lidded basket for miscellanous items like hot-water bottles and spare soaps. It can be easier to assess this once you've done an initial clearout, as you can see what you actually need to store.

Allocate people their individual 'zones' If you're sharing the space with other people, agree a storage system and give them a zone each.

Put the remaining objects away You should be left with just the 'Keep' objects. Start to allocate them to your storage solutions, taking account of usability, accessibility and visibility. For example, put ones you'll use a lot (such as deodorant or moisturiser) in accessible areas as opposed to those used less frequently (such as sun cream).

The bathroom giveaway list

When you survey your bathroom, you may be thinking, 'There's not much to get rid of'. However, look a little closer and you'll find there's probably plenty! Here's a blitz list:

• Out-of-date medication – return these to a pharmacy or surgery to dispose of safely.

- Out-of-date cosmetics (see opposite).
- Hotel miniatures and sample sachets that you aren't going to get round to using.
- Old magazines or books you never read.
- Old toothbrushes (these should be replaced every three months).
- Old hair brushes (throw away if the nubs on the end of the bristles are missing).
- Unnecessary duplicates.
- Random bottles and containers.
- Contact lens cases (these should be replaced every three months).
- Sponges, loofahs and bath puffs (replace every 4–6 weeks).
- Open tampons (if the plastic packaging has torn, they could be exposed to bacteria).
- Kids' bath toys that aren't ever used or have gone mouldy.

Bathroom storage solutions

Storage typically needs to cover toiletries, cosmetics, bathroom cleaners and bulky towels. It needs to be easy to access, able to withstand water exposure and to contain multiple bottles and pots without them getting lost in the throng. Here are some suggestions:

Clear cosmetics organisers are a great way of storing cosmetics and make-up brushes so you can see what you've got without having to dig around. They also stop them rolling around or toppling over.

Shelf risers can be put into bathroom cabinets to help you maximise space: short jars and pots can go underneath while taller bottles and sprays can go on top.

Stackable plastic baskets are a perfect under-sink solution to keep bottles such as cleaning products tidy without them falling over and spilling, as well as being easy to wipe clean.

Storage bins with cut-out handles make for a transportable box so you can easily move important products to wherever you need to in your home.

Overdoor hook racks are a way of keeping towels and dressing gowns from congregating on the floor. Each household member can have a dedicated hook.

Shower caddies and shelves help to keep shower essentials such as shampoo and soap accessible, neat and tidy. Suction varieties or ones that slip over the showerhead are available if you aren't able to secure one to the wall.

Shelf-life of cosmetics and toiletries

How do you know how long your beauty products will last for? It's worth having a regular product purge. The best indicator is either the 'Expiry date' (printed on the box or container) or the 'Period after opening' (PAO) which usually has a jar symbol with a number of months after it (e.g. 18M means you can use it for 18 months after opening). However, there are some general guidelines for how long products will safely last after opening:

• Natural and organic products – up to 6 months
• Bath gel, shampoo, conditioner – 2 to 3 years
• Perfumes and aftershaves – up to 3 years
• Shaving cream – 2 years
• Shaving loofahs and sponges – 4 weeks for natural, 7 weeks for synthetic

• Toothpaste – 2 years
• Teeth-whitening strips – 1 year
• Sun products – 1 year (but one season)
• Powders (including blusher or eyeshadow powders) – 1 to 3 years
• Foundation in a jar or a cream powder – 1 to 3 years
• Liquid foundation (in tubes or jars with dispenser) – 1 year
• Nail polish – 1 year
• Lipstick and lip gloss – 1 year
• Pencil (eye or lip) – about 1 year
• Skincare products in sealed packet with pump – about 1 year
• Skincare products in jar – 6 to 10 months
• Solid eyeliner and eyebrow pencil – 6 to 8 months
• Bronzer – about 6 months
• Mascara – 3 to 6 months
• Liquid eyeliner – 3 to 4 months

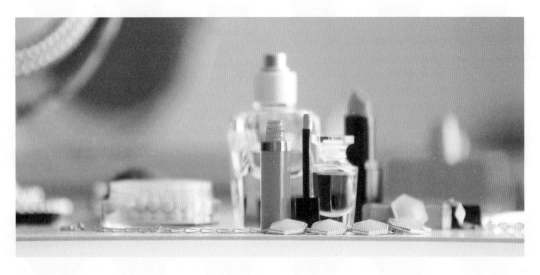

Kitchen and utility spaces

The kitchen is where we spend the most time when we're at home, according to research. It's the hub of the house, the place kids pile into for after-school snacks and to do their homework, where friends gather to drink tea or G&T, and where we prepare and eat meals to celebrate, commiserate or simply live.

For all these reasons and more, our kitchens are 'hero' spaces that have to work well for us. However, this also makes them a place where clutter can gather and turn order into chaos. As the hub of the house, the kitchen can often be a dumping ground for all manner of random things, from junk mail to children's artwork and shower gel that hasn't yet made it upstairs. Here's how to get more order and organisation into your kitchen:

Quick tidy or big clear-up? Use the 'Allocating time' section (pages 64–65) to work out what amount of time you have, whether it's

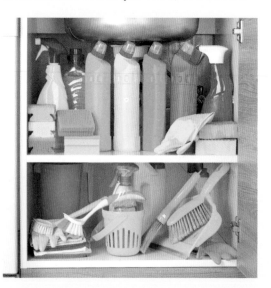

10, 20 or 30 minutes, or something longer like a half-day or a full-day. This will help you manage your expectations. Treat your kitchen and utility areas as two different spaces to tackle.

Do the washing-up Wash up or load (or unpack) the dishwasher; you'll be surprised how ready to tidy it will make you feel. It's a way of psychologically defining the start of tidying. If the breakfast things are in the way, you'll start off feeling everything is chaotic.

Create your 'Sort it' zones This will help to keep you focused and enable you to start assigning items to specific categories from the outset.

Decide what storage you're going to need Think what is most practical in the way of shelves, cupboards, cabinets and containers, and where they are best placed for convenient access. Some suggestions are given overleaf.

Assess all units and drawers It may be that you only have a few cupboards to open or perhaps you've got row upon row of long-forgotten cabinet drawers. Before you start pulling everything out just open them up and take a good look at what you see. Don't forget high up, low down and hidden spots.

Decide what will live where Whether it's an open shelf, a cupboard or a drawer, think how you would ideally use the space in your kitchen. For example, where do you keep the kettle? It makes sense to keep mugs, tea and coffee close by. Items you use a lot need to go in easy-to-access places whereas those you use only occasionally can be stowed away (these might go in the 'Relocate' pile if, for example, they're going to the utility room or cellar). Don't start putting anything back yet.

Empty one cupboard and drawer at a time It may be tempting to pull everything out at once but unless you've got a tiny kitchen you could end up with no room to actually sort anything as well as possibly demotivating yourself. Clear one out, then start populating your 'Sort it' piles. Go through the process for each cupboard and then for each drawer. Think about how you can reduce, reuse or recycle when you're assessing all the items.

'Do I really need it?' As you sort, keep referring to the five questions on page 67 to keep you on track. Check the 'Kitchen and utility spaces giveaway list' overleaf as a prompt for items you may want to blitz.

Throw away out-of-date products You'd be surprised how dates come and go and you find yourself the owner of five-year-old food colouring! Research shows that out of an average of 57 kitchen cupboard items, 13 are out of date. Products that are still in date which you aren't likely to use can be put in the 'Give away' pile. Some could be suitable for local food banks (see Resources).

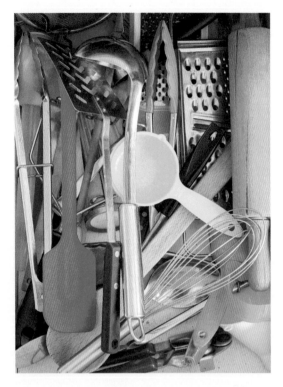

Clear the decks Remove items from the Give Away, Recycle or Bin 'Sort it' zones and set them aside regularly so you have more physical and psychological space for the items you're keeping.

Allocate people their individual 'zones' If you're sharing the space with other people, agree a storage system and give them a zone each (such as a shelf in a cupboard or the fridge or space in the freezer) and tell them they now have a part to play in keeping it tidy.

Put things away When the cupboards are emptied, and you have your 'Sort it' piles ready, you can start to allocate your 'Keep' items to your storage solutions, taking account of whether they'll be sufficiently visible, accessible and usable.

Kitchen and utility giveaway list

Sheila Chandra, author of *Banish Clutter Forever*, says that 'Kitchens tend to collect dreams and aspirations about our domestic selves.' In other words, they are often full of things that would be perfect if we ever got round to being a 'domestic goddess' or had that fantasy oversized country kitchen. Utility spaces aren't much better: they can easily become a dumping ground for objects to organise later, only to discover 'later' never comes.

Here are a few suggestions. It's not an exhaustive list; the key thing is to look critically at the individual objects and prepare to be ruthless.

• Electrical 'white elephants' such as rice cookers, bread makers, smoothie-making bullets, if you never take them out and are more likely to use something instead (like a saucepan for rice).

• Excess plastic containers (how many do you really use, even if the lids do fit?).

• Used 'once in a blue moon' gadgets such as melon ballers, mezzalunas, egg cubers, milk frothers and corn-on-the-cob holders.

• Inherited retro items you'll probably never use, from fondue sets through to hot plates.

• Out-of-date products.

• Cookery books you never use, and don't feel especially inspired by.

• Crockery, pots and cutlery you don't like and never use.

• Damaged and broken items.

• Nearly-empty products, bottles and containers you aren't likely to finish up.

Kitchen and utility storage solutions

There is a wide range of great storage solutions to help you inject order and organisation into your kitchen spaces.

Space-saving devices There are heaps of these to help you make the most of your kitchen space. For example, shelf risers are a good way to double up on space, while tiered shelving increases tidiness and stops bottles and jars getting lost in the back of cupboards. Pull-out pantry cupboards that slide into the room give more storage in a small space. Turntables prevent you having to root around in the back of cupboards for pans or jars.

Fridge organisers From containers and fridge trays to clever organisers to prevent drinks cans rolling around the place, there are plenty of fridge storage solutions out there. These organisers will also help reduce food wastage by stopping foodstuffs disappearing amidst fridge chaos.

Cupboard organisers These range from plastic container tidies and undershelf stemware holders for organising wine glasses through to vertical and horizontal plate racks and stick-up trays and shelves to pop on the inside of cupboard doors.

Drawer organisers are ideal for keeping cutlery and utensils tidy, as well as accessories such as kitchen foil.

Transparent stackable containers Stackable means they're space-saving; transparent means you won't have to second-guess what's inside or faff around with labelling. Keeping tidy is easy with modular containers.

Sink organisers Sink caddies for sponges, scrubbers, soap bars and other cleaning items help to keep sink areas clutter-free. Clever under-sink storage can turn this often neglected (and chaotic!) space into one where you can find essentials with ease.

Hanging organisers If you don't have enough storage from cupboards, shelving and drawers, it may be time to start hanging things. Whether it's overdoor rails or racks, wall grids with hooks or a ceiling rack for pots and pans, make the most of dead space in your kitchen.

Extra shelves A wall plate rack and mug tree can be a way of storing crockery for easy access. Look for potential space where an extra shelf can go, perhaps above a window.

Utility spaces Dedicate a shelf or cupboard for laundry products close to your washing machine, making sure they are out of the reach of children and pets.

If you have the space, invest in a series of baskets for the clothes of each member of the household to be put in when they come out of the dryer or off the clothesline for them to put away themselves. Keep an odd socks basket for rogue single socks and gloves so that they can stay there until they are reunited with their mate.

An empty pocket box dedicated to objects you take out of pockets before you put them in the wash means people will know where to look if they're missing something.

Kids' spaces

Whether it's a bedroom or a playroom, kids' spaces have a tendency to be a magnet for clutter. Open the door of an average child's room and you'll find yourself tripping over toys, party gifts, books, dressing-up outfits and clothing.

Playrooms and kids' bedrooms are, typically, where entropy (chaos) and inertia (things don't move unless you move them) are demonstrated at their finest! We all know how keeping this chaos under control can be a constant battle so here's how to inject some much-needed order and organisation, and also involve the kids.

Decide what storage you need Bearing in mind how the room is going to be used, assess the likely storage requirements, whether shelves, cupboards or boxes – there are some suggestions overleaf.

Lay down your 'Sort it' cards Clear a big area in the middle of the floor and allocate your 'Sort it' zones. This will help to keep you focused and enable you to start assigning items to their various categories from the outset.

Create an 'odds and ends' box Small bits of plastic seem to accumulate in every

children's space, whether it's a cracker prize, pieces of Playmobil or Lego, or a counter from a board game. It may be tempting to just chuck them out, but you might not know just how crucial that piece of plastic is. Put the ones you aren't sure about in an 'odds and ends' box and go through with your child afterwards to check it's not a precious item; a temporary stop-gap while you make sure it's not the crucial missing part of a game or toy.

Start populating your 'Sort it' piles Clear out cupboards, drawers, shelves and trunks, and put everything in the middle of the floor to allocate to your 'Sort it' sections. For example, are there any items that can be put in the 'Give away' pile? They could be repurpose as a school raffle prize or given away to charities who need toys and children's clothes. Are you planning another baby or know someone who is? Some of your sorted items may need to be stored for later use…

'Do I really need it?' Keep referring to the five questions on page 67 to keep you and your kids on track when making decisions as you sort. Check the 'Kids' spaces giveaway list' overleaf for items you can safely blitz. Think about how you can reduce, reuse or recycle when you're dealing with these items.

Remove items that aren't staying in the room When you've sorted the last object, remove items that are going elsewhere, namely those in the 'Give away', 'Recycle', 'Relocate' and 'Action' piles. Keep 'Special objects' in the room because some of them

Safety is paramount
Make sure bookcases or cabinets can't topple over or unbalance when drawers are pulled out, and can't be swung or hung from; standing furniture should be safely secured to the wall. Heavy objects should be at floor level so children don't pull them on top of themselves. Make sure a child can't climb into a cupboard or chest and close the lid or get stuck.

may end up staying there (and others might go in a memory box).

Allocate people their individual 'zones' If your children are sharing the space, agree a storage system that works for all of them. This may involve them having a zone, shelf or drawer each – if they have a say in the system they're more likely to abide by it.

Put the remaining objects away You should be left with just the 'Keep' objects. Start to allocate them to your storage solutions, taking account of usability, accessibility and visibility. For example, put ones you'll use a lot in accessible areas as opposed to those used less frequently. This will make it easier for children to have some independence about what they are planning to play with.

Deal with 'Special' or nostalgic items These will be from the 'Special items' clearing zone and should be dealt with last so you don't get distracted by them. Some will go straight back onto a shelf or chest but some may be destined for a memory box (like a framed

picture of their newborn footprints – a small child may be happy to display it but it might cramp a teenager's style!). See pages 50–53 for more about managing nostalgia.

Get your kids involved

It is good to involve kids in all aspects of tidying – what to keep and chuck away, then how to keep things tidy on a day-to-day basis. Many of us have childhood memories of prized possessions being spirited away by overzealous clutter-clearing adults. This is likely to be because we weren't involved in the clearing or tidying process and weren't able to contribute our thoughts and our effort when it really mattered. Although as adults we can probably understand why our parents wanted us out of

the way, getting kids on board and willing to subscribe to tidying is a good thing to do.

Tidiness may benefit their mental health Not only does sorting out kids' spaces make sense from an organisational standpoint, it could also have positive psychological benefits, too. Professional declutterer Vicky Silverthorn says, 'Psychologists tell us that our children are increasingly stressed and anxious, and I believe that chaos in their rooms and playrooms can often be part of the problem.' Tidying up will provide physical clarity – and possibly mental clarity, too.

Tidiness is a skill for life Where possible, it's best to get your kids involved in tidying up and helping them to understand the importance of both clearing and tidying.

You'll be equipping them with invaluable skills for life – skills like keeping tidy, being organised and also being able to let go of objects so they're not weighed down.

Remind that tidying is a 'constant' 'But I did it the other day!' is a refrain that many adults hear from kids. As you'll no doubt explain, they may well have tidied last weekend but the order has gone and it needs doing again. Tidiness is a 'constant', like walking the puppy or watering the lawn. Explain that there are daily habits (such as making their bed, putting toys away and putting dirty clothes in the laundry basket) and weekly ones (such as a big toy tidy-up) that need to be done. Tell older kids about 'inertia' to explain why it isn't going to happen by itself!

Make tidiness an easy habit to keep to Let the process be an easy one, minimising anything that's likely to distract or hold things up. Label drawers and tubs so they can put their own clothes and toys away; have a laundry basket in their bedroom (or show them where the family basket is kept). Good storage systems are helpful for everyone.

Make tidying fun! This may be about 'spin' but human beings, big or tiny, are more likely to complete a task if it's fun rather than boring and laborious. Definitions of 'fun' will depend on the age of your children. For younger ones, you might turn tidying into a game, such as 'Who can find all the toys that are yellow?', whereas for older ones the incentive might be playing on their console when the task is complete. Older kids might also fancy selling their unwanted things for extra pocket money, when you ask them to do a clearout session.

Keep fiddly toys tidy with a blanket

If you want to avoid having to scoop up Lego or other multi-piece toys at the end of a play session, tip it out onto a large blanket or sheet first, before they start playing. That way the kids can have fun and all you have to do when they're done is lift the four corners of the fabric and tip the items into the storage box or basket.

Kids' spaces giveaway list

• Old computer consoles and games
• DVDs & CDs, and players
• Clothes they've grown out of (including dressing-up outfits).
• Soft toys they've grown out of (they are allowed to keep favourites, of course).
• Broken toys or ones they no longer use (e.g no longer age-appropriate).
• Toys, games or puzzles with pieces missing (and which aren't in the 'Odds and Ends' box!).
• Duplicate toys and games.
• Furniture they've grown out of (e.g. changing tables or too-small chairs).

Kids' spaces storage solutions

There's virtually no end to the types of storage you can buy for children's spaces, though you will have to assess whether it's practical or decorative. As with all storage solutions, it's a case of assessing what space you're working with, what you're hoping to store, how old the children are and how they use the space. This will impact the storage you opt for – and how you utilise it, too. Here are some storage suggestions.

Novelty storage systems From fairy-themed hanging units for dressing-up essentials through to storage units with built-in play areas, these may not stand the test of time: that fireman theme feels like it will last forever but it never does! However, novelty solutions can be a brilliant way of helping your child to see tidying as fun rather than a chore.

Modular storage system Add to this as and when you need it and you'll have a system that should take them from baby up to when they're considering university. Consider incorporating cubby holes for boxes or baskets, hanging space for clothes, drawers for accessories, and shelves for displaying favourite toys, moneyboxes or photographs.

Storage chests with drawers These are effectively mini chests of drawers that are

great for tiny things that children often collect, like sequins, stickers and scented erasers. Within each drawer you can put an insert to compartmentalise the space.

Book storage Somewhere for books is essential, whether it's a freestanding bookcase, a forward-facing book display unit or in a book storage cart. Research shows that reading for pleasure gives children confidence and is a powerful factor in their progress later in life.

Well-labelled storage Whether it's solid colour boxes or transparent storage, labelling with words, pictures or both will help kids to understand that everything has a home and that's where it needs to be returned to! See-through storage is an additional prompt

to enable kids to see what toy type is stored in them without having to pull off all the lids.

Hooks You can never have too many hooks in kids' spaces but don't forget to put some low down so they can actually reach them. Commando hooks are a great way of creating impromptu hanging space – put them on the wall for kids to hang necklaces, bracelets and lanyards from.

Crafting cart This is such a practical piece of kit, ideal for housing all the crafting paraphernalia such as felt-tips, pencils, paints, scissors, glitter and glue. Being able to wheel it from one space to the next also means they can craft wherever they want to (including outside) and when they've finished you can wheel the cart out of view!

Sleeping and dressing spaces

Of all the rooms in our home, the place we sleep should be a haven of relaxation where we can separate ourselves from the distractions of life. It therefore needs to be tidy and clutter-free for peace of mind.

Research shows that one in three of us go to a bedroom to unwind, with nearly 15 per cent of us saying it's the only place we can get some peace and quiet. But what has tidiness got to do with this? A study at New York's St Lawrence University found that if you have a messy bedroom, you're more likely to get a poorer night's sleep and have increased anxiety – plenty of reason to get things in order. Some of this chaos is from having too many clothes. A survey in 2018 found that British women have 558 million unworn items in their drawers and wardrobes (men have 223 million), adding up to £10b in wasted spending or £200 per adult. The research also discovered that women wear only 55 per cent of the clothes they own. Reducing your own clothing count will release a lot of space, and you probably won't notice what has gone. Here's how to achieve a more organised personal space.

Try this: Sort your hanging clothes by length. This will enable you to use the space underneath the shorter items for additional storage, such as stacking drawers or a trunk.

Quick tidy or Spring clean? Work out how much time you've got. If you want to completely tidy my bedroom, you'll probably need to dedicate a full day to it or more.

Decide what storage you're going to need Bearing in mind how the room is going to be used, assess what your storage needs and solutions are likely to be.

Lay down your 'Sort it' cards Clear the area in the middle of the floor and place your zone labels. This will help to keep you focused and enable you to start assigning items to specific categories right away. Have binliners at the ready for 'Giveaway', 'Recycle' and 'Bin'. Allocating clothes to them straight away will stop you having a change of heart – out of sight, out of mind.

Begin sorting Start with, say, your chest of drawers and sort each drawer, then move on to the wardrobe, shelves and trunks. The items are probably already in category groups within the various locations. Allocate them to the 'Sort it' piles as you go.

'Do I really need it?' Keep referring to the five questions on page 67 to keep you on track when making decisions as you sort. Think about how you can reduce, reuse or recycle.

Remove items that aren't staying in the room When you've sorted the last object, remove items that are going elsewhere, namely the 'Give away', 'Recycle', 'Relocate' and 'Action' piles. Keep 'Special objects' in the room because some may end up staying there (others might go in a memory box). If you can, go straight away to your chosen local charity shop with the designated 'Give away' and 'Recycle' clothes and shoes.

Allocate people their individual 'zones' If you share your sleeping/dressing space with someone else, agree on a system that you're both happy with. This may involve rejigging an existing system if it isn't quite working for you or, indeed, considering different storage solutions altogether.

Put your 'Keep' objects away Start to allocate them to your existing or new storage solutions. Take a fresh view on how you want to designate drawers and cupboards, perhaps by type of clothing, perhaps by how regularly you use them. Some people keep seasonal winter and summer clothing separate, packing one set away.

Deal with 'Special' or nostalgic items These will be from the 'Special items' clearing zone

Use adjustable shoe shelves
If you're installing shoe storage, choose shelves where you can adjust the height. Flat shoes only take up around two to three inches of space but your heels or wedges may be up to eight inches high – that's some difference! Store shoes heel to toe if you need to liberate space.

and should be dealt with last so you don't get distracted by them. They may be clothes with personal significance that you don't wear any more, they may be special trinkets or decorative objects. Some will go straight back onto a shelf but some may be destined for a memory box or attic storage.

Getting rid of clothes
For some people it's really easy but for the rest of us it can be a trial.

Be pragmatic As many as one in ten of us hang on to unworn clothes in case they come back in fashion, or we are hopeful that we will fit it again one day. However, if you've not worn or used something for two years, the likelihood is you don't really want or need it, or you would purchase something else.

Be resourceful Your rejects could delight someone else. Sell off your unwanted stuff online or in yard or car boot sales.

Be kind Charities always want quality donations. Instead of a visible reminder of your shopping errors, clear out some space and do some good for others in the process.

Other items to move out of a bedroom

Piles of books We all have a 'I'll get round to it soon' book pile. In Japan there's even a word for it: tsundoku. Have the book you're reading on your nightstand and no more.

Exercise equipment Your bedroom should be a haven, not somewhere that reminds you of all the things you aren't achieving right now – such as getting into an exercise regime.

Anything work-related 8 in 10 of us admit to working from bed and yet two-thirds of us suffer from disrupted sleep. Part of 'sleep hygiene' is removing objects that distract.

Sleeping and dressing space giveaway list

• Clothes and shoes that don't fit (too big or too small, or that hang awkwardly when on).

Vacuum-sealed storage bags

These allow you to store clothes you're not currently using, such as winter clothes during the summer. Air is drawn out with a vacuum cleaner, compressing the contents to make the bag airtight.

• Clothes and accessories you don't like.

• Items that are broken, ripped or stained.

• Clothes you are keeping for nostalgic reasons but never wear, or which you always plan to wear – but never do.

• Specialised sportswear that you don't use.

• Unwanted gifts, jewellery and toiletries.

• Bedding that is worn, ripped or stained.

Storage solutions

Under-bed storage There's so much space lurking beneath your mattress, it makes total sense to make use of it from a storage point of view. Invest in a storage bed with drawers that pull out or a mattress that lifts up, or add boxes or drawers on castors. If your bed is too low for rigid storage, try soft boxes that you can manoeuvre under with ease or raise your bed a few crucial centimetres with bed risers.

Drawer organisers are essential if you want to maintain order in your bedroom drawers. They come in various configurations including small boxes or compartments for underwear, tights and socks through to larger ones for bigger items such as t-shirts and sweaters. Buy adjustable or expandable organisers to adapt to your changing needs.

Dresser-top organisers A dressing table or the top of a chest of drawers where you put make-up, jewellery, fragrance bottles and the contents of your pockets, can easily descend into chaos. Boxes with their own compartments – such as dedicated stacking make-up organisers – will bring harmony to the space, as will jewellery stands and hair dryer/flat iron holders.

Shoe storage There are various ways you can store your shoe collection. Transparent drawer-fronted boxes which house a pair of shoes (or several pairs of flip-flops) can stack up in a cupboard or closet and enable you to see what shoes you've got at a glance. A behind-the-door shoe organiser is another great option to store pumps and sliders.

Hanging spaces Tidy rails provide you with a portable solution for housing clothes on hangers and so much more – especially useful if you are a renter or need a moveable storage solution. Build on it by adding hanging shelves into the mix, including slim ones for shoes and wider ones for sweaters, t-shirts and trousers. Whatever hanging space you've got, use velvet hangers which are thin (so you can store plenty of them) and non-slip so clothes will stay put and remain tidy. Organise smaller items with special scarf holders, belt hangers and handbag hooks.

Other bedroom storage Useful options could include night stands and blanket boxes. Night stands or bedside tables come in all kinds of configurations, including ones with drawers, cupboard doors or shelves. Nonetheless, although drawers and small storage spaces sound ideal for stowing your things, don't fall foul of stashing not-needed items just because there's space for them. (When you tidy your bedroom, tackle these hidden spaces, too.) Blanket boxes and trunks often fit perfectly at the end of a bed and are great for stowing bulky items like bedspreads, duvets and even towels.

Frisk your clothes for cash!

Before you give any clothes or bags away, don't forget to empty pockets. You may find things you love in there – or money!

Living spaces

Lounges and living rooms are where we engage (apparently) in an average of seven activities each month, from watching TV and having a nap through to playing a musical instrument, eating a takeaway and even dancing.

Living rooms are one of the busiest areas of the home, used by all household members (and that can include pets!) and therefore tend to get easily disordered. A tidiness system supported by hard-working storage solutions is vital to stop this high-activity space falling into chaos. The space needs to balance comfort and practicality, so you can rest, work and play in a stress-free way.

Ask yourself 'How is the room used?' It might be just for sitting and watching TV but research suggests it'll be for so much more than that. Does it house a home office or a children's play area? If it does, deal with those as separate entities, one at a time.
Decide what storage you're going to need
Bearing in mind how the room is going to be used helps you assess what kind of storage

solutions you need. There are some starter suggestions overleaf to help.

Quick tidy or big clear-up? Work out what amount of time you have, whether it's 10, 20 or 30 minutes, or something longer like a half-day or a full-day. This will help you manage your expectations of what can be achieved in each session.

Lay down your 'Sort it' cards Clear an area on the floor with the zone labels in front of you. This will help to keep you focused and enable you to start assigning items to specific categories from the outset.

Clear out cupboards, drawers and shelves Put everything in the middle of the floor and start populating your 'Sort it' piles. It's highly likely that your 'Relocate' pile will grow most

quickly as you repatriate items that have gravitated towards this much-used living space.

'Do I really need it?' Keep referring to the five questions on page 67 to keep you on track when making decisions as you sort. Check

The home library

A 2014 survey looked at how people arrange their bookshelves and it would seem we crave some kind of order. Sorting books by genre was the most popular, followed by alphabetically by author, then totally randomly. Sorting by size and colour also featured.

the Living spaces giveaway list for items you can safely blitz. Think about what you can reduce, reuse or recycle.

Remove items that aren't staying in the room When you've sorted the last object, remove items that are going elsewhere, namely those in the 'Give away', 'Recycle', 'Relocate', 'File' and 'Action' piles.

Allocate people their individual 'zones' If children or other adults are sharing the space, agree a storage system that works for all of them. This may involve them having a zone, shelf or drawer each.

Put the remaining objects away You should be left with just the 'Keep' objects and 'Special items'. Start to allocate 'Keep' items to your storage solutions, taking account of usability, accessibility and visibility. For example, put items you'll use a lot in accessible areas as opposed to those used less frequently.

Deal with 'Special' or nostalgic items These are best dealt with last so you don't get distracted by them. Some, such as trophies, photos or other special mementoes, might go straight back onto a shelf or display surface. Others may be stowed in a memory box or stored for posterity.

Living spaces giveaway list
• Dead plants (if they're still alive but unhappy, put them in the 'Relocate' pile).
• Old magazines.
• Unwanted books (ones you've already read, will never read or don't need).

• Soft furnishings that are stained, become threadbare or motheaten, or cushions that have gone soggy and bumpy.

• CDs, DVDs and video tapes that are out of date or you no longer use.

• Old appliances and wires (e.g. for out-of-date phones or devices) that you can't or don't use.

• Spent reed diffusers, candles and plug-in air fresheners.

• Decorative items that you don't like.

Living spaces storage solutions

Bookcases and shelves are an absolute must for most living spaces. They could be part of a modular unit incorporating other features such as magazine racks, drawers and cupboards.

Sideboards, cabinets and media units with doors enable you to neatly store possessions like paperwork and files without having to constantly clap eyes on them, as well as giving you surfaces for decorative touches such as lamps and framed photographs.

Drinks trolleys and bar carts have had a resurgence in popularity in the past few years and are the perfect way to keep bottles and glasses stylishly tidy.

Ottomans and storage chests are particularly useful if you've got objects like toys that you want to quickly stow, for example when people drop by, or for bedding if you have a sofa bed in the room.

Coffee table with integrated storage A lift-top table with storage underneath, or with shelving under, is a nifty take on this living room staple. Be inventive by using an old trunk, a large mending box or even a large food hamper. Use organisers inside to keep order and to stop it being a dumping ground.

Home office

Whether you have a dedicated home working office, a small zone in a room where you do paperwork, or an area where your admin seems to gather, chances are it's a space in need of some order and organisation.

Some of us are lucky enough to have home office space just used by ourselves. However, with space at a premium, it's likely we'll be sharing it with others, whether a partner, or a teen studying for exams. If so, get them involved in the tidy, find out what their storage needs are too, and get some tidying rules in place.

Quick tidy or big clear-up? Decide what time to allocate to your tidying task, bearing in mind that you might need to peruse papers while deciding how to sort, file and bin them.

Tidy fact

We carry out adminstrative tasks most days. Whether it's sorting out insurance, paying off credit cards or checking bank accounts, renewing licences and permits, booking appointments and more, the average adult carries out 109 'life admin' tasks every year, research has revealed. A tidy home office will help to streamline the inevitable.

Lay down your 'Sort it' cards This will help to keep you focused and start assigning items to specific categories from the outset. Have binliners at the ready for 'Giveaway', 'Recycle' and 'Bin/Dispose'. Your 'File', 'Action' and 'Shredding' sections are likely to play centre stage in this home office tidy.

Decide what storage you're going to need Bearing in mind how the space is used, and how big it is and what furniture and storage

options are realistic, assess what your storage needs are. This might include filing boxes, folders and inserts – there are suggestions overleaf and specific storage needs may emerge as you go along.

Clear out cupboards, drawers and shelves Put everything in the middle of the floor with your 'Sort it' sections, including stationery, paperwork and files. Clear pinboards, too, as these are also clutter magnets.

'Do I really need it?' Keep referring to the five questions on page 67 to keep you on track when making decisions as you sort. Check the Home office giveaway list overleaf for items you can safely blitz. Think about how you can reduce, reuse or recycle when you're dealing with these items. See the section on Resources at the back of the book for ways to recycle home office items.

Remove items that aren't staying in the room When you've sorted the last object, remove the items that are going elsewhere, namely those in the 'Give away', 'Recycle', and 'Relocate' piles. This will help to clear both physical and mental space. 'File' and 'Action' should stay to be sorted, as should 'Keep' and 'Special objects'.

Put the remaining objects away Start to allocate 'Keep' items to your storage solutions, taking account of usability, accessibility and visibility. For example, documents you need to access quickly and without fuss (such as passports) should be easy to access while previous tax return documents can go in a file storage box to be kept on a high shelf or even stored away in another room like an attic.

Deal with File and Action items Sit with your pile of items and start to sort them NOW. It may be tempting to leave them – especially if your tidying has been arduous – but you'll find the pile will start growing within a day if you don't. Another tip: don't place 'Action' items in a horizontal in-tray as this will encourage piling rather than filing. A vertical magazine box with dividers allows for initial sorting out, and means you can actually get to the paperwork without having to leaf through too much.

Deal with 'Special' or nostalgic items These should be dealt with last so you don't get distracted by them. Some, such as old letters and cards, photos or other mementos, might be go straight back onto a shelf or pinned on a notice board. Others may be stowed in a memory box.

Try this: Go see-thru

Transparent acrylic desk and drawer accessories mean you can easily see what you've got (quickly locating a blue rather than a black pen, for example), which means it should be easier to keep on top of keeping them replenished as well as clearing out duplicates and what you don't need.

Home office giveaway list

• Old mobiles or cellphones (some charities like to have these; do remove sim cards and delete data before disposing).

• Old chargers and wires.

• Old cameras (if they are classic models, they might even have some value or interest).

• Magazines and newspapers.

• Dead stationery, e.g pens that don't work or are drying out, broken pencils, dried glue.

• **Documents to bin**: product manuals (they can be found online); catalogues, brochures; receipts that don't have a tax purpose.

• **Documents to shred**: Expired documents; ATM receipts; bank deposit and withdrawal slips; cancelled cheques; utility bills and personal bills as soon as they are paid, if you don't need them for expenses or for tax.

How long should I keep paperwork for?

Personal information Keep passports, ID and driving licences; birth, marriage, divorce and death certificates; HMRC and NHS details (in the UK); health insurance details; wills and letters of attorney; certificates of professional qualifications; pension documents.

Bank, credit card and loan statements This will vary depending on which country you live in. In the UK, HMRC suggest 22 months after the end of the tax year or roughly six years if you run a company. Contact your tax office if you need further information.

Utility and personal bills A year. This includes phone, electricity, gas and water bills.

Warranties and receipts Until they expire (keep important receipts for six years).

Insurance documents. Until you take out a new policy.

Payslips Keep monthly payslips and any documentation relating to pay given to you from the government (such as P60s).

Medical information Your doctor should have these but you may well need your own copies to hand so keep them indefinitely.

Home office spaces storage solutions

Document letter tray This is to house your 'inbox' and your 'current projects'. We may be trying to reduce the paperwork that infiltrates our daily lives but some is still inevitable. A physical inbox is where bills, letters and other 'to do' project paperwork goes when you've opened the post. However, it doesn't stay there: it's a holding area until it gets dealt with or filed. Deal with it as soon as you can and no more than once a week to avoid paper overload. Current projects are those that are active and ongoing and not yet ready to be filed.

Recycling paper basket and trash basket These are two separate items because you should be aiming to recycle as much paper waste

Try this: Ink out your name

If you don't have a shredder to dispose of confidential paperwork, use a special rolling ink stamp to cover up important information on the document such as bank balance, account numbers, address and full name or date of birth.

as possible. Another option is a basket with separate compartments for different kinds of waste. Anything confidential should be put through a shredder.

Filing cabinet We challenge anyone to stay truly organised without some kind of filing system. Even a single-person household will accumulate enough paperwork and 'must keep' objects to warrant at least one expanding fan file. However, you won't regret investing in a small filing cabinet, and a lockable box for more private items.

Drawer organisers Compartmentalised boxes that slip into drawers are an office space essential. Drawing pins, staples, erasers and paperclips all have to live somewhere.

Desk tidies From handy places to store pens, remote controls, calculators and magazines, there is a wide range of desktop storage solutions. Search 'desk organisers' online to see some of the options to meet your needs.

Tidy technology solutions Keep cords tidy and tangle-free with cord keepers/cable clamps and consider a tech shelf (complete with holes for chargers) above your desk so you always know where to find them.

Joining spaces

These spaces – which include hallways, corridors and utility areas – tend to be high-traffic zones where people dump things with wanton abandon! They are also places no-one tends to claim ownership over, or responsibility for tidying.

Your hallway is the first thing any visitor will see so it's worth giving your tidiness regime some thought. Here are some tips on how to keep them tidy and clutter-free.

Allocate time and 'Sort it' labels Decide what time you have for this space and create your 'Sort it' categories. There may not be objects for each one but all sorts of rogue items make their way into joining spaces!

Ask yourself 'How is this space used?' If it's a hallway or corridor, who uses it and what do they do in there – is it where people collect and take off coats, shoes and other accessories? Do they dump skateboards and scooters (or bicycles) there despite your protestations?

Decide what storage you're going to need. Assess what storage solutions best fit your needs. Do you need an accessible (but safe)

place for keys and bags. Will you need a space for shoes and coats, and wet things. To encourage children to be tidier in the hallway, you'll need low hooks and boxes.

Start populating your 'Sort it' piles Clear out cupboards and shelves, take things out of boxes and off hooks. Put everything in the middle of the floor with your 'Sort it' zones. It's highly likely that your 'Relocate' pile will grow quickly as you repatriate items that have gravitated to this much-used space.

Remove or store the objects Remove the items that are going elsewhere. Start to allocate 'Keep' items to your storage solutions, taking account of usability, accessibility and visibility. Agree a storage system that works for everyone. This may involve each person having a drawer or peg/rail, or have designated areas for certain kinds of item.

Joining spaces giveaway list

• Junk mail, old newspapers and magazines.
• Coats, shoes, hats, scarves, gloves and umbrellas that are damaged or too small, or which are never used or worn.

Get into the post-opening habit

Open letters straight away to avoid them piling up. Decide if it is for filing, actioning or recycling. Procrastinating with your post will have a knock-on effect on your general filing tidiness whereas tackling it as soon as it arrives should become a keystone habit.

Joining spaces storage solutions

Coat storage Your choice for storing outerwear will be influenced by how much space you have and how many of you are using it. Options include freestanding coat stands, coat racks against the wall (many of which have shelves or cubbyholes underneath for shoes or accessories) or hooks. Another great option is a luggage rack which integrates hooks with a shelf for hats, bags and boxes. Remember, if you've got kids, install hooks at their height, too.

Shoe storage A dedicated shoe locker, a shoe cabinet or a wall-mounted shoe rack will help to store shoes and boots in an orderly fashion. Choose a low shoe locker to double up as a bench, or a bench with a lift-up lid to store shoes, equipment and accessories.

Shelf for keys and post Whether it's the top of a radiator, a console unit or a shallow shelf, somewhere to put keys and post is essential when it comes to hall orderliness. However, see it as a 'landing pad' rather than a permanent home for anything. Deeper shelves above head height are another way of creating extra storage space in a hall.

Attics and cellars

When did you last head up the ladder to your attic or loft or down the creaky stairs to your cellar or basement? Among the least-visited spaces in our homes, they're also the most likely to be filled with junk.

Challenge yourself to recall exactly what's in your attic or cellar, if you have either, and you may struggle beyond the basics. If you're lucky enough to also have under the stairs as a storage option, there's plenty stowed out of sight here too. Some people are so averse to clearing out these spaces that when they move, they simply transport the whole lot with them, junk and all. However, a comprehensive sort-out along with a few storage solutions can help to make these areas a tidy and workable part of your home.

'Can I get to it?'

If your items are hard to access, you're creating a barrier that will stop you getting to them at any point in the future. Make it as easy as possible to get what you need again, or you'll lose the benefit of all the sorting-out.

Is your attic storage-ready?

Before you even begin to think about tidying your attic, you need to ask yourself three fundamental questions. If the answer to any of these is 'no', you need to address them before your attic is ready to be used to store your belongings.

Is it accessible? Is it easy to get into the attic in the first place or does it involve a treacherous ascent? Most attics are accessed by ladder so the crucial question here is, 'Is it secure?'. Statistics show that around 48,000 people in the UK each year attend A&E following a ladder accident at home and the main reason is the ladder slipping due to the user overreaching or because the ladder hasn't been properly secured. At the very least, a firmly screwed-down ladder or pull-down steps are vital if

you're going to use your attic safely. Adding a handrail is also advisable.

Is it safe? Attic safety may start with the ladder but it doesn't stop there. An attic can be a hazardous place, a dark void with patchy floors or no floor at all, slim joists to pick your way across, not to mention nails or beams to catch you and your head by surprise. If your attic isn't already boarded, this is the first thing to do to before it can be used for storage.

Lighting is also vital so you're not having to venture up there with a torch – poor lighting means poor safety, especially if there are beams to contend with. If there is limited headroom, you may need to put wadding on them to avoid any collisions.

Is it temperate? Your attic is accessible and safe – but is the storage environment up to scratch? Whereas cellars and basements tend to be damp or moist, attics are often dry (unless your roof is leaking). However, even though your belongings might stay dry, they are likely to be exposed to extremes of temperature; very hot in the summer and very cold in the winter. Before you put something up there, think about whether it

The attic rule

Attics are best for items you don't need that often. If you need them just once or twice a year, put them up in the loft.

needs to be stored in a more temperate space, particularly delicate items such as artwork, electronic equipment or computers.

Quick tidy or big clear-up? In reality, unless your attic is already ordered and organised, you're likely to need a good chunk of time to sort it. You're unlikely to achieve very much in less than an hour and much more likely to make headway with a half-day or full-day.

Break it up into geographical 'zones' If your attic or basement is brimming with boxes and bags, knowing where to start may be a trial. Make a plan, for example, when you go up into the attic, to start your tidy on the left-hand side and work your way round clockwise through different zones. Work with a similar principle in your cellar.

Create your 'Sort it' zones Create these away from the room in question, whether it's an attic or a cellar. Even the cleanest attic and basements can be dusty and hot, or with low lighting, so sorting things in there might not be fun. Besides, much of what you're sorting will be leaving the house – thrown away, given away or repatriated – so they may as well come down sooner rather than later! If your basement or loft is big, however, you may decide to do the sorting there.

Sketch out a storage plan Unless you know where you're putting things, when you repopulate your attic, chances are you'll forget where everything is. Draw a plan of what is going where – summer clothes, winter clothes, archived toys, for example – so you know what lives where. Allocate

What belongs in the attic
- Seasonal festive decorations.
- Memory boxes and family heirlooms.
- Items you use only occasionally such as ski gear or toboggans.
- Suitcases and backpacks.
- Camping gear.
- (Sorted) personal items belonging to children who have moved out.
- Seasonal clothes (in airtight bags).

areas to individuals if need be. This 'road map' will help you to locate everything later.

Label like crazy! As you put everything away, you may think you'll never forget what's in that box, but in reality you'll probably have forgotten in just a month's time. Along with your storage plan, labelling means you'll know exactly what is where.

Decide what storage you're going to need It may be that as you sort, you'll discover your storage needs alter slightly. However, deciding what you need before you begin enables you to sort in situ once you know what's going and what's staying. See the storage suggestions overleaf for ideas.

Work through a couple of boxes or bags at a time It's quite demotivating to be surrounded by a gazillion containers to sort through – anyone who has moved will know this. Also, you're unlikely to be able to sort your attic out in a day so tipping everything out means you're giving yourself unnecessary work at the end of each tidying session.

Start populating your 'Sort it' piles Depending on the last time you ventured into your attic or basement, this could be a lengthy process. But don't be demotivated. Do it a bit at a time, working through each box or container and focusing on that, rather than thinking about the next box to tackle.

'Do I really need it?' As you sort, keep referring to the five questions on page 67 to keep you on track when making decisions. Think about how you can reduce, reuse or recycle, and check the Attics and cellars giveaway list below for items you may want to blitz.

Clear the decks Remove items regularly from the 'Give Away', 'Recycle' or 'Dispose/Bin' zones and set them aside so you have more physical and psychological space for the items you're keeping.

Put things away Start to allocate your 'Keep' items to your storage solutions, labelling them and taking account of whether they'll be visible and accessible.

Attics and cellars giveaway list

These large storage spaces help us to cultivate a 'out of sight, out of mind' mentality towards our possessions. However, there's something psychologically burdensome about keeping hold of so many items that, in all honesty, we couldn't even recognise in a line-up! Here's what should go during your attic or cellar sort-out:

Items you've decluttered from the rest of the house Tempting though it may be to transfer into the attic or cellar anything you're not sure whether to keep or not, you should resist the lure. All you're doing is storing them to sort out for another day.

Anything that's broken or past its best Be honest: if it was worth fixing, you'd have done it by now. Each year or month that goes by makes it less and less likely that you'll mend that broken lamp or bedside table. Now is the time for it to go.

Old household items Whether it's furniture, soft furnishings such as curtains or paintings you've inherited but aren't sure of, now is the time to get rid of them. If they were really useful, you'd be using them by now. Household gadgets such as a vacuum cleaner you're keeping 'just in case' can also be given away.

What belongs in the cellar

• Items you're going to use only occasionally but more than twice a year.

• Anything flammable such as camping gas canisters and cleaning products but don't stow these anywhere near water heaters or boilers.

• Cans of paint. These need to stay cool as temperature changes can alter the colour so keep away from hot pipes.

• Anything too heavy to go in the attic.

• Cans of animal food but NOT bags. You're just inviting pests to visit!

• Bulk buys such as stacks of toilet and kitchen paper.

• Wine or beer, if the temperature suits.

Old tech Whether it's video recorders, TVs, laptops, smartphones or games consoles, technology moves on so quickly that by the time you've stumbled across them again, chances are they're obsolete. Also, fluctuations in temperature and moisture aren't good for electronics so if you're hoping they'll carry on working, store them somewhere more temperate.

Empty boxes When you buy a new electrical device, do you keep the box or packaging just in case you need to return it? It's time to throw them away, or put them into recycling. The same goes for instruction manuals – most are available online if you need them.

'Heavy heart' paperwork If it's non-essential documentation that brings back negative memories, allow yourself to bin it. If you need to keep a record of it in some way, simply scan or photograph it before you send it on its way.

Childhood artwork There's really no need to keep all your children's artwork from reception right through to college. Save a few key pieces for the memory box – and scan in or photograph the rest if you find it hard to let them go.

Anything you've well and truly forgotten about! If you've gone up to the attic or down to the basement and pulled something from a box, only to say, 'I'd forgotten about this!' it's probably time for it to go. If you can't even remember it, you're clearly not missing it. If the recollection is pleasurable or you'd like to keep it for the archive, do so, but it might be time to say farewell.

Attics and cellars storage solutions

These are the highest and lowest rooms in your home so are more prone to changes in temperature and moisture. Pests might find their way into these spaces and may go undetected until it's too late and they've eaten their way through your possessions. The storage you choose must reflect this.

Plastic boxes with tight lids Look for the word 'airtight' when buying these. A lid that fits but that lets air in could also let pests and damp in, too. They can also stack to make the most of vertical space.

Vacuum-sealed storage bags These are ideal for clothing, childhood soft toys and other fabric items that need to be protected from moths and damp. Put silica gel sachets in to reduce moisture.

Modular storage If you're working with an awkwardly shaped space, modular storage – including shelves that can be altered – could be the answer as you can build it to suit your needs. Shelves can fill an awkward corner, or utilise a sloping wall.

Wooden crate storage One economical way of creating low-level open modular-style shelving units is to stack empty plywood crates side-on, and use them to store smaller boxes.

Rafter hangers and hooks These can be useful for hanging light items, if well protected (keep coats in a sealed bag).

Have you got pests?

Noises Mice and rats are active at night so if you hear scuffling sounds up above when it's dark, this could be what's going on.

Chew marks and footprints If something has been chewed and it's not down to a domestic pet, it could be you have a resident rodent or two. Put some talc on the floor and inspect for footprints over the course of a few days.

Droppings You've definitely got rodents if you've found droppings. These tend to be found where there's food, which is why it's inadvisable to keep food anywhere but the kitchen or in airtight storage elsewhere.

Moths! You'll know you've got them when you see one flying around (there's no such thing as 'one moth'…) and discover holes in your clothes or soft furnishings. The most common clothes moths are small and pale silvery brown and fly around when it's warm. The best way of killing adults, eggs and larvae is to deep freeze clothing at −18°C (−0.4°F) for at least two weeks. There are some proprietory moth repellers you can buy to hang in wardrobes and put into stored boxes and trunks. Rugs, carpets and upholstery can be treated with insecticide, in a commercial freezer or carried out by reputable companies.

How to deal with photographs

We've touched on this already with the discussion about managing nostalgic items (see pages 50–53) but it is worth a special focus as it is such an emotional minefield for many, in terms of what you keep and what you let go.

The question of stored family photographs – and other personal history – follows on naturally from the process of tidying your attic or cellar, as this is where the archive inevitably ends up. Have you ever inherited or stumbled upon a box or suitcase filled with old family photographs or unidentifable collections of images and thought, 'How do I deal with this?'.

You could lovingly put them in albums so they're saved for posterity and are easy to look through. However, this process can be laborious, time-consuming and will take up just as much space or more when you're done. Besides, it's probably something you'll never actually get round to. So what should you do instead?

Antique family collections

Go through and save pictures that mean something to you Unless they already have names written on the back of them, chances are you won't know who's in the pictures, though you can also ask older members of your family. If you do know, write some details on the back yourself. Decide whether they are images you do want to keep and if so whether scans would be sufficient.

Donate them to a genealogist If there's someone in your family who enjoys looking into your family tree, give the pictures to them. They will no doubt be thrilled, especially if you're able to guide them through some of the faces and places contained within. You might find images of long-since changed places that could of be of interest to a local historical society.

Use a fast scanner If you use a flatbed scanner to scan in pictures, you could be doing it for hours – even days. A fast scanner can scan a picture a second so it's well worth the investment if you've got hundreds or even thousands of photos to get through.

Store photographs like a professional The National Archives recommends storing photographic prints flat and in chemically-

stable plastic or paper folders of pockets that are free from sulphur, acids and peroxides. These can be ordered from specialist photographic conservation suppliers. It also advises storing film-based negatives (single sheets or those cut into lengths of 4–6 frames) separately from other types of photographs, as they can produce acidic gases as they age.

Don't store them in the attic! Printed photographs and negatives are best kept in the coolest, driest part of your home where there isn't a big fluctuation in temperatures. In other words, not in your attic, cellar or garage (which is exactly where they often end up). Humidity can cause them to stick together and too much heat could fade and degrade them, as will direct light of course. The best place is an interior cupboard that isn't adjacent to an outside wall. If it has to be in an attic, put them in an airtight box and check regularly to ensure they're free of dust, dirt and insects.

What about all your own photographs?
Pictures stored in old albums, in old negative sheets, stored on CDs and discs, in digital cameras (many now out of date), not to mention the countless images on smartphones and computers – how to manage these is an overwhelming challenge in itself. To locate, consolidate, identify and label – and curate – your pictures is the kind of project that could be never-ending, and is something you might never get to (even when you retire!). Some rationalisation is necessary, so that you don't feel overwhelmed but can keep some track of images created over time and are able to access the important ones. Creating a routine and system for this, perhaps setting aside an hour a month or weekend a year, might help, whether this is uploading new (labelled) images to a shared space in chronological order, or working back through batches of historical images to organise and identify them.

Gardens and outdoor spaces

When it comes to tidiness, gardens and outdoor spaces are just as important as inside ones. However, sheds, garages and other 'out of sight, out of mind' storage areas can quickly become a chaotic dumping ground for objects that don't have a proper place inside the house.

A tidier outdoor space is an inviting one, and you are more likely to use and enjoy it. An organised space is also easier to manage; for example, if it suddenly starts to rain, if objects such as cushions and throws have a designated storage space they can be cleared away without fuss.

Many of us see gardens as an 'extra room' so there's no reason why they shouldn't be given the same tidiness treatment as the rest of the home. Here are some tips on how to bring order to gardens and outdoor areas (both front and back), garages and sheds.

Look at the weather Check the forecast before you start hauling objects out of sheds and garages for your clear-up. A tidying session in dry weather will be less of task than if it's raining. Also, good weather will allow you to lay objects on the patio or an outside table without having to jettison the task half-way through.

Quick tidy or big clear-up? See the Allocating time section on pages 64–5 to work out how much time you have to spare, whether it's 10, 20 or 30 minutes, or even a half-day or a full-day, weather permitting.

Lay down your 'Sort it' cards This will help to keep you focused and enable you to start assigning items to specific categories from the outset. The most likely ones will be 'Give away', 'Recycle', 'Dispose/Bin', 'Keep' and 'Relocate', but you may even have things to file if you have seed packets that you want to store away.

Ask yourself 'How is this space used?' Who uses it and what do they do in it? Is the garden or backyard a family space? Do you have a garden room and, if so, is it used as a home office or workshop or is it a den for the

Shed sort-out

Almost a third of us admit that we can't get into our sheds because they're too crammed full of equipment and other possessions – time to have a tidy!

teenagers? You may well find your outdoor space has different zones and therefore serves a multitude of functions. If you use the space for outdoor entertaining, you might want a shed or section of your garage dedicated to accessories such as a barbecue, cooking utensils and paraphernalia such as cushions and parasols. If you've got kids' garden toys, you might want to put them somewhere that's easily accessible for children to get out by themselves. Make a note of each area and how it is used (e.g. does the entrance to your outside room need a rack for muddy shoes) and you'll soon start to see what your storage needs are.

Clear everything out and start sorting Leave no stone unturned. Put everything in your designated clearing space with your 'Sort it' sections in front of you. Once you've done this, start allocating everything, right down to the last terracotta pot, football and stray ball of gardening twine.

'Do I really need it?' Keep referring to the five questions on page 67 to keep you on track when making decisions as you sort and check the Garden and outdoor spaces giveaway list below for items you can safely blitz. Think about how you can repurpose, reuse or recycle objects elsewhere in your home or that someone else might have a use for.

Remove items that aren't staying When you've sorted the last object, bag up or box any that are going elsewhere and remove them from the outside space. This should leave you with your 'Keep' pile.

Put the remaining objects away Start to allocate 'Keep' items to their designated space, taking account of usability, accessibility and visibility. For example, put things you'll use a lot in accessible areas as opposed to those used less frequently. Share the storage plan with others.

Garden and outdoor spaces giveaway list

• Broken or unwanted children's toys (such as trikes and inflatable toys).
• Broken, rusty or unwanted tools and garden accessories.

• Mouldy or motheaten fabric items such as cushions or deckchairs.
• Unused old cans of paint and other decorating items.
• Unused bikes (one of the most common items kept in sheds).
• Unused plant pots, flower pots and seed trays.

Garden and outdoor spaces storage solutions

Sheds There are a wide variety of shed types and sizes, from small ones without windows to larger, glazed ones that are roomy enough to store lawnmowers and even garden furniture. Depending on your needs, you can line them with shelves, storage organiser sets (for screws and other bits), rails, and hooks for storing pots, planters and tools. A wall holder with clips to hold rakes, brooms and other handled tools will keep them ordered and also prevent them from being stepped on by mistake and causing injury.
Tool or bike shed Ideal for storing bikes, obviously, but also if your outdoor space won't comfortably permit you to have a

A place for every tool

If your shed is being used for tool storage, a pegboard is a great way to stow hammers, spanners and other DIY essentials. Trace round each tool with a thick felt-tip so you know exactly where every tool lives.

Lock your shed for safety

Don't forget to add a lock to your shed to keep belongings protected from burglars. It will also help to keep children and animals out if you're keeping hazardous items such as weedkiller and sharp-edged equipment in there.

full-depth shed, a tool or bike shed is a skinnier option that still gives plenty of storage. For example, where a 1.2 x 1.8m (4ft x 6ft) shed gives you around 144 cubic metres (5000 cubic feet) of storage, a 0.9 x 0.2m (3ft x 2ft) tool shed still provides a capacious quarter of that whilst barely encroaching on your overall outside space.

Garden storage bags are a handy way of transporting items to different areas of the garden, such as toys and cushions, and can be easily carted back into storage when done. Some might double up as camping-style seats.

Storage furniture A large outdoor sofa or chunky coffee table may look like a space luxury but if you choose one that has cushions or tops that lift off to reveal plenty of storage you're onto a winner. Not only is storage furniture a great solution for extending comfort into your garden, it is also a clever way to stow objects you need but don't necessarily want to see, such as barbecue covers and hot tub accessories. A win-win garden storage solution.

Shed culture

Of course, for many a shed is no longer simply a place for stowing rusty bicycle wheels, rarely-used garden equipment and objects that haven't found their natural place in the home. Research shows that 40 per cent of us also head to them as a place to get away from the stresses of work and family life. What exactly are we doing in our sheds? Almost four in ten of us have turned them into a hobby or craft room while seven per cent of us work or run a business from there (author Roald Dahl wrote his books in his shed, inspired by seeing the writing shed of Dylan Thomas in south Wales). And for many of us – more than one in ten – our sheds are simply a place to wind down by reading, listening to the radio or watching TV.

Garden rooms and summer houses If you've got the space, a garden room is an unrivalled way of making your outside area usable all year round – as well as giving you extra space for housing or storing bigger items such as garden tables, sofas or even a pool table, or other items that need to be protected from the elements.

Garden storage boxes These are deceptively roomy and are great for piling toys and games in, such as badminton nets and racquets, or soft furnishings such as blankets and cushions. They also double up as extra seating: just put a padded cushion on top. Available in a variety of materials, a polypropylene one will withstand even the harshest winters, as well as keeping contents dry.

Unwanted tools? Recycle them

Many of us have old tools and equipment lying around, unused. Instead of chucking them away, contact a charity that will collect and overhaul them before making them into comprehensive gardening kits for needy recipients, often around the world.

Not surprisingly these outside sheds can begin to resemble an overcrowded room inside the house. You might need to also follow the tidying tips and advice suggested for interior home offices and living spaces to help bring order into your exterior home-from-home.

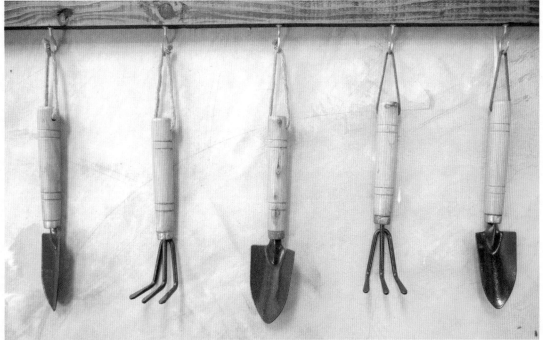

Garages

Nearly half of us whose homes have a garage don't actually use them for storing a vehicle. Instead, they're typically filled with bicycles, sports gear, gardening equipment, DIY items and household clutter instead.

If your car is parked elsewhere, there's no harm in a garage being used for additional storage. The key is making it work for you, rather than letting it descend into chaos. Here are some garage tidiness tips to help you make the most of the space.

Garage tidiness DO's:

• If you are parking a car in the garage, create a clear area around it so it's less likely to get damaged if a paint pot falls from a shelf or by bicycles being brought in and out.

• Free up valuable floor space by making the most of the walls and ceiling for storage. Use plyboard to create shelving in otherwise unused space, for items you aren't so likely to need. Wall-mounted racks or tracks with adjustable fittings mean you can hang sports equipment and tools so they're easily accessible, rather than ending up in tangled piles in corners.

• Hoist systems and bike hangers are a

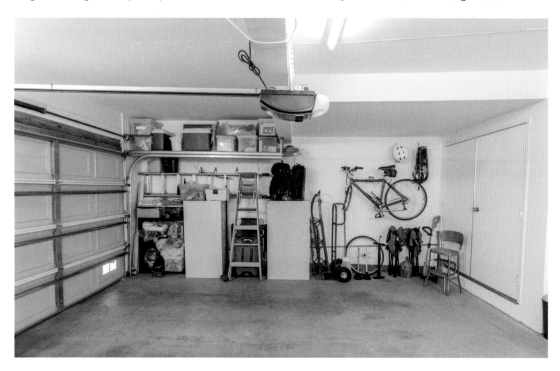

good way to free up floor space. Bike shops sell hooks that you can mount on the wall or ceiling joists to keep them out of the way.

• Think accessibility. Objects you use a lot, such as recycling boxes, need to be as close to your garage door as possible whereas objects you rarely use, such as ladders or picnic boxes, don't need to be quite so easy to reach in a hurry.

• Store objects in plastic boxes with lids rather than cardboard ones. This will make possessions less likely to be affected by pests such as rodents as well as protecting them from damp.

• Choose storage that is safely secured to the wall. If you load rickety shelves with heavy objects such as tools, tins of food or household items such as cleaning products, they'll be unstable and could tip over.

• Choose shelving (preferably metal, which can withstand damper environments better than wood) that is tall but isn't too deep so that you can maximise space but objects don't get 'lost' in the depths of them.

• Buy lockable cabinets for both valuables and dangerous items such as chemicals.

• Store similar items together so they're easier to locate. For example, have distinct areas for tools, gardening equipment, sports kit and household items.

Garage tidiness DON'TS:

• Store flammable items within half a metre of a boiler or heater.

• Keep valuable or perishable items in there. Garages tend to be colder than the rest of the

home, and may also be damp, so anything sentimental should be stored elsewhere for safety.

• Make shelving so high that the garage doors can't open…

• Cover up drains, fuse boxes or ventilation with storage.

• Exceed the uniform distributed load (UDL) levels of your shelves (this is how much weight can be safely stored on each shelf section, details of which should come with the shelves).

What's in our garages?

It's interesting to learn what is typically kept in garages: DIY tools 76 per cent; decorating equipment 67 per cent; gardening equipment 64 per cent; sports and gym equipment 49 per cent; scrap wood 42 per cent; fridges and freezers 35 per cent; stored food and drink 25 per cent; shoes and coats 18 per cent; motorbikes 10 per cent.

Cars and bags

You've worked through your home, from top to bottom. What is possibly left to tidy? There are places allied to the home – satellites, if you like – such as your car or even your handbag that could also benefit from the clearing process. Organising these can help you to feel even more in control.

Tidying cars

Research shows that just under one-third of us stow away objects in our vehicles for months at a time and a quarter of us regularly lose items in them. It's time for a clear-out. So what's the drill?

Empty everything out

The first thing to do is to take everything out of your car, including from the boot or trunk, seat back pockets and all the glove compartments and side pockets. You're unlikely to need the usual range of 'Sort it' piles for your car. Instead, three piles should do, namely:

Tip: If your seats have airbags, make sure you don't place anything like a hanging organiser over them.

- Items to bin.
- Items to keep in the car.
- Items to put in the house or garage.

When you're deciding what to keep in the car, your aim should be to ensure the car is as uncluttered as possible. Plan to keep only the essentials. Nothing should hinder the comfort of anyone using the vehicle.

Decide what to keep in your car

Most of us probably don't even think about essentials we should keep in our cars, but there are a few practical basics:

- Hazard triangle.
- Hi-vis jacket or vest.
- Breakdown service contact details.
- Insurance company contact details.
- Spare tyre/jack, and jump leads.
- Replacement bulbs and fuses.
- Car charger for your mobile or cellphone.
- Road map(s).
- First-aid kit.

- Water.
- Non-perishable food.
- Loose change.
- Umbrella or waterproof clothing.

Create a place to put rubbish

One in ten people admit to leaving things to fester in their car for a year or more. After you've had a clearout, decide upon a designated space for collecting rubbish while people are in the car. This could be anything from a plastic bag through to a specially designed car bin. Get in the habit of emptying the bin every time you fill up.

Car storage solutions

Glove compartment Keep only the essentials in here, such as important documents (insurance documents and roadside assistant information), users' manual, torch, phone charger, and pen and notepad.

Seat and boot organisers With a range of storage compartments, these help to keep your car tidy – especially handy in a family vehicle. Many include mesh pockets to keep items in view and to house anything from bottles, drinks, tissues and toys through to magazines, guidebooks, ipads or tablets. These come in the form of back seat organisers, simply hooking over the front seat, as well as containers that slip in between the seat and gearstick.

Plastic box Keep a box in your boot or trunk for the essentials listed above; you could also keep a list in a plastic wallet so you can audit what is there.

Tidying handbags

It isn't just our homes that are getting in the way of us reaching our tidiness goals. Research shows that one-third of women spend an average of 81 days of their lives rooting through their handbags trying to find things. What's the key to a tidy handbag?

Take everything out That includes all pockets, pouches and compartments both internally and externally. You'll be surprised at what you find lurking in a rarely used zipped inside pocket. Tip it upside down and shake out everything; use a lint roller for that extra level.

Have a chuck-out Throw away all obvious rubbish and clutter including old receipts, tissues and odd bits of paper. Get rid of multiples, too; you only need one pen.

Audit what you need Before you add items back in, have a good think about what value they add. Ask yourself 'Is it worth the space?' and 'Is it worth the weight?' If the answer to either of these is 'No', leave it out.

What belongs in your bag?

Don't be swayed by 'just in case' mentality. Be ruthless or you'll find your bag descends into chaos as soon as you've put everything back. Here's the list of important things:

- Keys.
- Money and credit/debit cards.
- Phone and charger/power pack.
- Driving licence.
- A few personal care items.
- Medication.
- Pen and small notebook.
- Reading glasses and sunglasses.

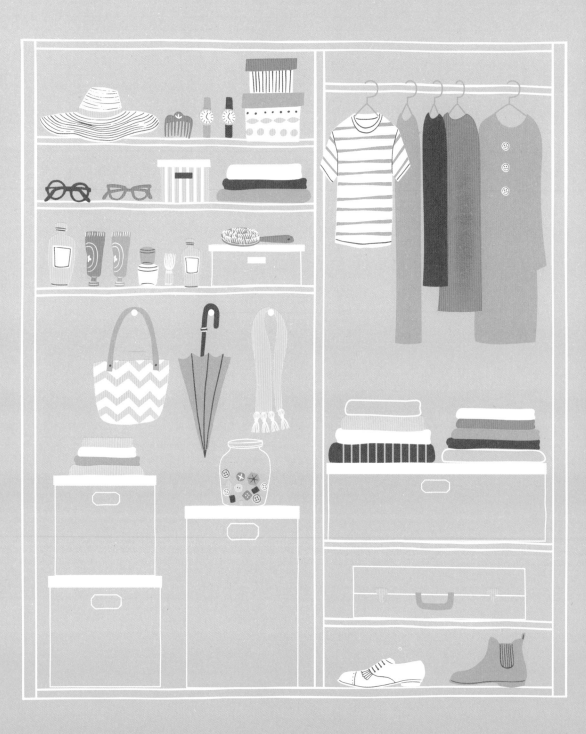

STAYING *Tidy*

Six rules for permanent tidiness

Once you've done your big tidy and have your calm clear spaces, you want to maintain them and enjoy the ongoing benefits of all your hard work. It is important to create a system that works for you. Here are six good guidelines.

It's all very well someone telling you, 'This is how I do it', but if their tidying technique doesn't suit you it won't work. Find a routine that suits your day to day realities.

Make your tidiness intentions known

Part of keeping on top of things is to get other people to subscribe to it by telling them about your intentions. Not only will this help to hold you accountable (if someone is likely to ask 'Have you started tidying yet?' you're more likely to do it) but it will also alert them to the fact that you're trying not to accumulate 'things' anymore.

Be kind to yourself as you tidy

Tidying isn't just a physical act – it can be a really emotional one, too. The process may well tug at your heart and feel like it's pulling you backwards at times. This is only to be expected so don't give yourself a hard time over it. Some tidying processes are going to be tougher than others. Learning to embrace being 'good enough' and understanding that the 'perfect is the enemy of the good' will help you to beat inertia by realising that a little bit counts for a lot. We can be so fixated on doing something perfectly that we end up not doing it at all.

Keep things because you love them – not just like them

'Like' simply isn't enough when you're deciding to keep or clear out. Do the objects you own give you pleasure and happiness, and a feeling you couldn't be without them? That's 'love'. Respect your belongings and your relationship with them. Whether you're keeping, donating or binning, owning objects shows they probably meant something to you at some point so be mindful when you decide what to do with them. Realise that nostalgia isn't a bad thing (the past can shape and inform who we are today) but that it may need management so you're not bogged down by it.

Get into the 'reduce, reuse, recycle, hire, borrow' frame of mind

It's so easy to find yourself buying things because it's immediate, they're cheap or even being given away for free. Instead of recluttering, there are various ways of repurposing what you've got or owning temporarily instead. Hiring and renting is a great option. Similarly, don't see shedding things as permission to buy new things; the aim is to reduce adding to our possessions without due consideration.

Gather 'experiences' instead of things

This may be a departure of habit for many of us, but if you begin to embrace the gathering of experiences rather than objects we can guarantee you'll start to feel a whole lot lighter, both physically and psychologically. When someone asks you what you want for your birthday, perhaps you can suggest a ticket for a theatre trip or a gig, a class, a spa treatment or simply ask for time with a friend. Objects come and go but experiences stay with you for life. Say no to freebies and inherited objects, too, as it's not about the cost of them but the space they will take up. Perhaps you will start to view your role as more a custodian of objects that are passing through your life and which then will move onto someone else.

Keep on top of tidying

Do something every day to prevent 'rebound'. Don't leave washing up overnight, clear the decks of daily clutter at the end of each day, and make your bed every morning (this is a well-known keystone habit). Put clothes back in their place or in the laundry and never let this creep over the top of the laundry basket. As soon as you take clothes off a clothes horse, off the line or out of the tumble dryer, fold or hang them and put them away. When it comes to paperwork, you should aim to do it once a week, setting a minimum of half an hour a week to file it. Remember to open your post as it arrives, too. Set aside a regular time to make trips to the recycling station, council dump and charity shop.

Tidying myths – and tidying truths

Whether it's 'I might need it so I'm going to keep it' or 'I don't have time to be organised', tidying myths abound. Here we examine why they're wrong (and holding you back from tidiness) and offer some ways through.

Myth: 'I don't need to tidy every day'
Truth: Marie Kondo says that 'Tidying is a special event' and that you shouldn't do it every day. However, as we've seen from The science of tidiness on pages 14–15, disorder is a natural state of being and we have to put constant work in to keep things from descending into chaos. Even if this means just putting shoes thrown off back in the hall or putting the recycling out, a little every day will help to keep things ticking over. See your 'special event' tidy as something you're going to enjoy, knowing your 'little and often' helps things to stay ordered.

The 'do I really need it?' checklist

Here are some questions to ask yourself before you buy something new. It will help you to glean whether you really need it or not.

• What do I own that is similar?
• Who do I know that owns one already?
• Where will I store it if I decide to keep it?
• Why do I want it?
• When will I use and maintain it?

Myth: 'I need to tidy by category or it won't work'
Truth: The premise is that we store items from the same category – say, books – in different places and if we tidy room by room we can't accurately assess what we've got. However, most of us have sufficient memory to be able to say, 'I've just found two screwdrivers in the utility room and I know for a fact there are more in the garden shed.' The benefit of tidying by location is knowing that at the end of your tidying session, you can tick a space or a room off your list.

Myth: 'I have to keep it if it's useful – even if I don't like it'
Truth: William Morris famously said, 'Have nothing in your houses that you do not know to be useful, or believe to be beautiful'. Preferably both! Some objects have no other use than being beautiful and we have talked a lot about those in this book. But what of an object that is useful but not that attractive? You may be tempted to keep it because you feel you should, but if you don't like it then you may be put off using it (and certainly displaying it) at all. It is okay to send items on their way to somewhere else where they can be used and appreciated.

Myth: 'I need to have everything tidy or I can't think straight'

Truth: For some people this is definitely the case but for others the imperative to have everything in its place before they can focus simply isn't there. Some of us are able to ignore the 'noise' of objects and get on with what we are doing. Some people even feel more creative if there are things around us. Author Alexandra Stoddard says: 'When I'm the happiest, my desk is not neat. It has lots of pens and the books I love. It gets messy when I'm in the flow.'

There's often a hierarchy of tidiness, where tidy people can feel that their 'way' is the only way and people who aren't tidy are simply waiting for an epiphany to start them on the way. Don't use tidiness or the lack of it as an excuse to get on with things, and decide for yourself whether you need more order, rather than the views of other people.

Myth: 'It's a waste to get rid of something that has some value'

Truth: These are often the hardest kind of possessions to part with. In a world where we are trying to be less wasteful and more resourceful, and are often watching our expenditure, it feels profligate to say goodbye to an item just because we don't like it. But why shouldn't we want to be surrounded by things we enjoy and love? If you don't like the aesthetic of something, give it away, or sell it and put the proceeds towards something you're happier with. That way you get to realise the item's value but can put the money into a replacement that will bring you pleasure.

As Marie Kondo says, 'To get rid of what you no longer need is neither wasteful nor shameful.' Don't feel bad about letting certain things go if they don't have personal meaning for you.

Tidiness resources

Whether you need new storage solutions for your sorted possessions, want to give cleared-out items away to worthy causes, or aim to sell unwanted items of value, here is a starter list of addresses to help you. (Note that companies come and go, and these examples are provided as suggestions not endorsements.)

Storage solutions

There are many places you can obtain great storage containers from, whether they're baskets, boxes, racks or rails. Ikea has branches across the globe (www.ikea.com) but whatever country you're in, there'll be other stores to furnish you with all the storage solutions you need.

www.argos.co.uk
www.theholdingcompany.co.uk
www.thewhitecompany.com
www.johnlewis.com
www.containerstore.com
www.lovethesign.com
www.meminio.com

Giving items away

You will be able to find many donation banks and charity stores for unwanted items, but here are a few suggestions.
Make-up and toiletries We all have make-up and toiletries we've received as unwanted gifts or used items we no longer need. There are charities that will take these and give them to people who will use them. For example 'Give and Make Up' is a charity founded by skincare expert Caroline Hirons.

It accepts all make-up and toiletry donations, new or used (except mascara and lip gloss which must be new), and supports women and children using women's refuge services (www.carolinehirons.com).

Old towels and blankets Some shelters and hostels might welcome these, if as-new. Animal rescue homes are also often desperate for towels, blankets and bedding. Contact them first to see what their needs are, www.dogstrust.org.uk.

Unwanted underwear Whether they're too small or you have too many, if you're wondering what to do with your 'gently worn' bras, there are organisations that will take them and do good with them. For example 'I Support The Girls' collects donations of new and slightly used bras (as well as individual sealed tampons and maxi pads) and distributes them to girls and women experiencing homelessness across the US and globally (www.isupportthegirls.org). 'Smalls for All' collects underwear for women and children in Africa, and accepts 'gently worn' bras, including sports and nursing bras (www.smallsforall.org). 'Against

Breast Cancer' collects via bra banks and for every tonne it collects it receives a good-sized donation towards its vital research (www.againstbreastcancer.org.uk).

Unwanted glasses: You might not need your old spectacles but they might be a lifesaver for someone else. Various organisations send glasses all over the world to those in need. For example 'Lions Clubs International' recycles old glasses for people who need them in communities across Africa, India and Eastern Europe. They have clubs worldwide (www.lionsclubs.org). 'Vision Aid Overseas' will put your old specs to good use to help the 10 per cent of the global population that are disabled because they don't have glasses. Visit the website (www.visionaidoverseas.org) or drop off at major optician's branches such as Vision Express and Specsavers.

Smart clothes Charity shops are always delighted to receive good-quality clothing donations to sell but there are other ways to put your unwanted items to good use. 'Dress For Success' is an international not-for-profit organisation that empowers women by providing professional clothing, development tools and a network of support to help them achieve economic independence (www.dressforsuccess.org). 'Smart Works' is a UK-based organisation that helps women get into the workplace by providing them with smart outfits, advice and support to give them confidence and self-

belief. Visit www.smartworks.org.uk to see what they'll take. 'Suited and Booted' has a similar set-up for men. Visit www.suitedbootedcentre.org.uk for further information.

Unwanted footwear As well as the smart clothes charities described above, 'Soles4souls' is an US-based charity that distributes donated shoes to people in need all around the world. They accept new and gently-worn footwear of all kinds from shoes, trainers and work boots through to flip-flops, sandals and dress shoes (www.soles4souls.org).

Computers, tablets and phones 'Computers for Charities' refurbs computers for charities and schools across the UK and further afield (www.computersforcharities.org). You may be due an upgrade, but that doesn't mean what you're getting rid of is worthless. 'IT Schools for Africa' sends refurbished IT equipment (from computers and laptops through to cables and keyboards) to Africa (www.itschoolsafrica.org).

Some charities make money by recycling old mobile and cellphones whether they're working or not. These include Mind, Oxfam, British Heart Foundation, Marie Curie and Age UK. Ask in your local charity shop for suggestions. Or, you can get the best price for selling unwanted mobiles and cellphones through comparison sites such as www.phones4cash.co.uk or www.sellmymobile.com. Wipe your data from the devices first.

Old tools 'Tools with a Mission' is a charity that collects unwanted tools, refurbishes and sorts them into trade kits, and sends them across the world to people who need them. Take a look at the 'Tools wanted list' on the website to see what they need (www.twam. uk). 'Workaid' is a charity that tackles poverty by supplying disadvantaged people with the tools they need to acquire practical skills and become self-supporting (www. workaid.org).

Household items Many charity shops accept small electrical items in good working order, but some have regulations against taking these; check before you bombard them with your unwanted items.

'The Furniture Re-use Network' supports more than 200 reuse charities helping vulnerable people in crisis. Visit the website to find out how to donate furniture, electrical appliances, IT equipment, paint, textiles, flooring and much more (www.reuse-network.org.uk).

Toy donations 'The Teddy Trust' collects cuddly soft animals and teddies from children around the UK and sends them to children suffering the traumas of war, starvation or abuse across the globe (www. teddytrust.org.uk). 'The Toy Project' recycles unwanted new and used toys and gives them to children who need them (www. thetoyproject.co.uk). Other charities include 'Stuffed Animals For Emergencies' (www. stuffedanimalsforemergencies.org).

Selling items

There are a number of ways you can sell your unwanted items, from the old-fashioned way of putting a postcard in a local store to selling online right across the globe.

• eBay is the go-to site for selling pretty much anything. When you're listing an item, try to schedule the bidding to close on a Sunday, which is eBay's busiest day of the week (www.ebay.co.uk).

• Gumtree (www.gumtree.com) is a classified website where you can advertise for free depending on the category and location.

• Facebook is a great option if you've got bulky items such as furniture or bundles of clothes and want to avoid postage. You can sell through local Facebook groups that are specific to certain locations, like cities or even your local community, or through Facebook Marketplace, which is like Gumtree or eBay (www.facebook.com).

• Etsy is jam-packed full of vintage objects so it's the go-to place for collectors looking to complete their collection (www.etsy.com).

• Rebelle is the place to head if you have designer clothes, shoes or accessories that you no longer want. You send them to Rebelle, which verifies the quality and authenticity of the item, then sells them for you (www.rebelle.com).

• Other resellers of clothing items and accessories include Depop (www.depop. com) and Vinted (www.vinted.co.uk). You can also sell objects through Preloved (www. preloved.co.uk) or Gadgetpanda (www. gadgetpanda.co.uk).

Recycling resources

If you want information on the 3Rs, you can find out more locally from your council or from an official government website. Check out charities that encourage local rehoming of all kinds of items, such as The Freecycle Network (www.freecycle.org).

Recycle Now is a Government-supported recycling campaign in the UK and has great online resources including a recycling locator (www.recyclenow.com).

The United States Environmental Protection Agency has information on how to reduce, reuse and recycle to help your community and environment (www.epa.gov).

'APDO', the Association of Professional Declutterers and Organisers, represents the UK decluttering and organising industry. It has an online directory to help UK clients find a local organiser to suit their particular organising and decluttering needs (www.apdo.co.uk).

Self-help organisations

Hoarding Disorders UK is the only UK-wide charity dedicated to supporting people affected by hoarding behaviours (www.hoardinguk.org). It helps and supports people who are affected not only by hoarding and clutter but also chronic disorganisation. They provide hands-on help within people's homes, using a person-centred approach to each individual (www.hoardingdisordersuk.org).

Index

This edition is published by Lorenz Books
an imprint of Anness Publishing Ltd
info@anness.com
www.lorenzbooks.com; www.annesspublishing.com

© Anness Publishing Ltd 2020

Publisher's note: Although the advice and information in this book are
believed to be accurate, neither the author nor the publisher can accept
legal responsibility or liability for any errors or omissions nor for any loss,
harm or injury that comes about from following advice in this book.

With thanks to Nigel Partridge for the design, and Shutterstock
for images.

ABOUT THE AUTHOR

Martha Roberts is an awardwinning journalist who has written
for national newspapers, magazines and websites, including
YOU magazine, The Sun, The Guardian, The Daily Mail and Psychologies,
where she has a monthly column. She is also
the author of *Shelfie: Clutter-clearing Idea*s published in 2018.